OUTTINGS
11.4.94
4 CIRCLE DR
NEWTON, KS

MIRROR of the MARTYRS

PURCHASED AT KAUFFMAN MUSEUM, NORTH NEWTON, KANSAS
WHILE VISITING THE MUSEUM THIS DAY WITH MY 2
DAUGHTERS, BETSY + SISSY (6 + 4 AGES). THE COPPER
PLATES BEGAN AS AN EXHIBIT AT KAUFFMAN IN THE LAST
12 MONTHS AND HAVE BEEN ON TOUR. I WENT ON THE
BOARD OF DIRECTORS OF THE MUSEUM THIS FALL.

MIRROR of the MARTYRS

Stories of courage, inspiringly retold, of 16th century
Anabaptists who gave their lives for their faith

John S. Oyer and Robert S. Kreider

Good Books
Intercourse, PA 17534

Acknowledgements

In the preparation of this book we are grateful for the counsel and assistance of many: Amos B. Hoover, Gary Waltner and Willy Hege; John Janzen, Reinhild Janzen, Robert Regier, Chuck Regier and staff of the Kauffman Museum, North Newton, Kansas; John D. Roth, Joe Springer and staff of the Mennonite Historical Library, Goshen, Indiana; Dale Schrag and staff of the Mennonite Library and Archives, North Newton, Kansas; Stanley Kaufman, printmaker; Alvin Hostetler, photographer; Phyllis and Merle Good and staff of Good Books; Ervin Beck, Mary Ellen Martin, James Juhnke, Mary Oyer, Mary Sprunger, Ruth Unrau and many more.

We owe much to the early gifts of sixteen patrons: Sam and Esther Bontrager, LaVerne and Luella Gerig, John Kreider, Robert and Lois Kreider, Mennonite Indemnity, Inc., Myrl Nofziger, Herbert and Louise Regier, Erie and Orlyss Sauder, Richard and Shirley Schiedel, Schowalter Foundation, Milo and Laura Shantz, Maurice and Opal Stahly, Elroy and Elberta Troyer, Leroy and Phyllis Troyer, Ora and Mary Troyer, and Dale and Irene Weaver. Add to this a major grant from the Kultusministerium of Rheinland-Pfalz, West Germany, and logistical assistance from the Mennonite Central Committee, Akron, Pennsylvania.

Robert S. Kreider,
John S. Oyer

International Bible Society: Holy Bible, New International Version (c 1973, 1978, 1984)— pages 23, 37, 41, 47, 49, 51, 53, 59, 61, 65. Reprinted with permission.

From The New English Bible. © The Delegates of the Oxford University Press and the Syndics of Cambridge University Press, 1961, 1970—page 43. Reprinted with permission. From The Revised English Bible, © The Delegates of the Oxford University Press and the Syndics of Cambridge University Press, 1989—pages 25, 27, 31, 55, 67, 69. Reprinted with permission.

Design by Dawn J. Ranck
Cover by Cheryl A. Benner

MIRROR OF THE MARTYRS

Published by Good Books, Intercourse, PA 17534

Table of Contents

Preface

For Mennonites in their 465 years of history, no book except the Bible has been more influential in perpetuating and nurturing their faith than the *Martyrs Mirror*. The treasured second edition of 1685 has been particularly prized for its 104 etchings by the gifted Mennonite artist Jan Luyken. Until recently the original 104 copper plates were thought to have been lost in the rubble of World War II.

In 1975, thirty plates appeared —straggling survivors of a 300-year odyssey. At that time, North American friends acquired seven plates, but twenty-three disappeared into the hands of a non-communicative Rhineland art collector.

In late May 1988 a phone call came. The twenty-three were available for sale. With gifts from sixteen patrons, the plates were purchased. As we claimed the *Martyrs Mirror* plates, the *Martyrs Mirror* claimed us.

Possession of the plates led to the creation of an inter-Mennonite trust, planning and designing of a mobile exhibit, writing and editing of a book-catalog, months of reading and research, preparation of educational materials, production of a cassette of sixteenth-century martyr hymns, fund-raising and crafting of an organization to facilitate a cluster of supportive projects. We have discovered that not only has this wonderful large book of stories captured our time and energies, but it has captured our minds and hearts.

From the receipt of that phone call in May 1988 our planning has been shaped by three concerns: first, this treasure of 300-year-old plates should be kept together, neither the prideful possession of one institution nor a scattering among many owners. The collection is held as an inter-Mennonite trust on behalf of all friends of the Anabaptist heritage. Hence, the assistance of the Mennonite Central Committee, Akron, Pennsylvania, was crucial in making that possible.

Second, these copper plates should be viewed as more than intriguing aging artifacts to be savored only by the few. These artistic works should instead be received gratefully as a conduit of a collective memory. Encompassed by the caring wings of story, a people nurtures and passes on its faith. These ancient plates offer an opportunity to tell in fresh ways how in perilous times the faithful followed Christ with joyful abandon.

Third, these old plates carry not a quaint, parochial tale, but a universal story. Although denying the practice publicly, many governments still carry out evil acts of torture. More prisoners of conscience languish now in lonely cells than in the 1500s. In the twentieth century more people have been killed for conscience sake than in any other century in history. The Anabaptist martyrs have kinship with a host of martyrs past and present.

This storybook catalog is designed both to accompany and enrich understanding of the exhibit, "Mirror of the Martyrs," but also to introduce the reader in word and image to the Anabaptist martyr experience.

Robert S. Kreider
North Newton, Kansas
and
John S. Oyer
Goshen, Indiana

Introduction

As modern persons reading Thieleman van Braght's *Martyrs Mirror* and studying Jan Luyken's etchings, we struggle to understand and find a vocabulary that gives meaning to this sprawling collection of martyr stories. The book eludes efforts at conventional analysis. We are drawn to metaphors in our search for meaning.

We Are in Awe

In these stories selected from the *Martyrs Mirror,* we come into the presence of several thousand Anabaptists who died as martyrs —more than any other group in the sixteenth century. Rulers demanded these radicals' exile or death for rejecting infant baptism.

Baptism for Anabaptists was a witness to a mature believer's voluntary faith covenant with God through Christ.

We are in the midst of a people who had child-like faith and yet were biblically wise. As we mingle among these Anabaptists, we hear them share a common core of beliefs: believer's baptism, authority of the scriptures, primacy of the New Testament, the discipleship of following Jesus, group discipline with compassion, living simply, separation of church and state, rejecting violence and war, and accepting the way of suffering and witnessing.

We See the Universal Sweep of the Martyr Theme

We marvel at the young editor Thieleman van Braght's majestic sweeping sense of history. For him, Christian history was the story of a martyr church. He begins with Jesus who was "born under the cross, brought up under the cross, walked under the cross and actually died on the cross."

Van Braght transcended parochial history to portray Anabaptist martyrs as actors in a universal drama. Tertullian, early church father, has best expressed the martyr theme in history: "The more ye mow us down, the more we grow, the blood of the martyrs is the seed of the church."

The early martyr church could not be crushed. It grew rapidly

A Christian Martyr Burned at the Stake, Polycarp 155

Proconsul: *"Swear by the genius of Caesar, repent, say: 'Away with the atheists!' . . . Swear, and I shall release you. Revile Christ."*

Polycarp: *"For 86 years have I served Him, and He has done me no wrong; how can I blaspheme my King who saved me?"*

—*Eusebius,* Ecclesiastical History

A Christian Tortured and Exiled, Origen
c. 200

Let us stand fast lest there arise in us any hesitation whether we should deny or confess.
— *Origen, writing to young Christians during the persecution of Septimius Severus, 193-211*

despite periodic waves of persecution. In van Braght we witness the church of the meek becoming the church of the powerful. A new emperor, Constantine (306–307), conquered Rome and embraced the Christian Church. He forged an alliance of religious and political establishments. Christians, once a minority, emerged a majority. Some Christians protested the new alliance of church and empire. The majority labelled the protesting minority as "heretics" and punished them with exile, torture and death. The once persecuted became the persecutors.

Was this then the triumph of the church or the fall of the church? Ever since Constantine, the choice between poverty and riches, lowliness and power has troubled the conscience of the church.

We Give Thanks

Three centuries ago, that busy young pastor van Braght gathered the martyr stories, searched city archives and wrote and edited a 1290 page volume. In his early thirties, van Braght saw his editorial calling as a ministry of passing on the faith. He wanted the *Martyrs Mirror* to be a means of recovering a virile, biblical faith for a generation softened by affluence and neglectful of a noble martyr heritage. "Read it again and again," he wrote. "Above all, fix your eyes upon the martyrs themselves . . . and follow their example." The story is told how he gave a copy of the *Martyrs Mirror* to his seven-year-old niece who was beginning to read. Faith incarnate in story.

We give thanks for the poet-artist Jan Luyken who lived close in time and spirit to the world of the Anabaptist martyrs. With his sensitive attention to detail, he opened windows of insight to the martyr stories: a chain on the ground—an intimation of cruel torture; the baker's freshly baked bread on the shelf; the curious dog on the fringes—Luyken's love for little creatures; the child watching bewildered as a parent is seized by the police. Luyken wedded image to word, thus illuminating our understanding of story.

We Are Captured by the Power of Image

We who pride ourselves on our tenacious fidelity to the printed word must be led by the *Martyrs Mirror* to reflect on this question: what has influenced us more profoundly, the 1290 pages of van Braght text or the 104 images of Luyken? Both are essential and complimentary. Here, unmistakably, image has particular persuasive power and communicative eloquence.

In a starkly simple etching of Dirk Willems rescuing his pursuer—hands of the enemy reaching out to the hands of the heretic—the word becomes flesh. More loaded with moral wisdom and conviction than a scholarly dissertation, this image captures the ethics of the cross.

We Sense the Mystery

The martyr stories of van Braght are fragmentary, wispy scraps of recorded memory. One's mind wanders off into the mysteries of what is not reported. Those who were close and heard the martyr's death hymn: how did they report the experience to their families? The executioner: how did he explain his vocation to his wife? What doubts lurked in the mind of the martyr? What remorse rumbled in the soul of the magistrate?

And who were the anonymous martyrs, of whom there were thousands? There were those "who dwelt in the untrodden ways" who held firm in torture, gave a "good witness," but no one was present to record their stories. And yet we discern their assurance that God "knows even when one sparrow falls."

We Hear a Song

The stories of the martyrs were first told person to person. A few stories were printed as broadsides and widely distributed. Early stories were sung as ballad hymns. Entries of a martyr's death in the *Hutterian Chronicle* often carry a notation such as this, "A song was written about him, which is still sung in the church." The martyrs came into the presence of death singing. In song they made their "good witness."

The earliest collection of martyr stories, *Het Offer des Herren,* 1562, named 135 martyrs in its hymn section, the *Liethoecxkn.*

The *Ausbund,* the Anabaptist hymnbook, 1564, contains fifty-three hymns written by Anabaptists imprisoned in the castle dungeon of Passau on the Danube. Many of the hymns tell stories of the martyrs.

It is intriguing to reflect how song can help fix a story in memory. Further, song seems to have a role in carrying story from the oral to the written. One is called to read the *Martyrs Mirror* as the psalmist, with an ear for the lyrical.

We Bring a Book Lover's Delight

The 1685 *Martyrs Mirror* reflected the state of the art in seventeenth century printing. The 1290-page, two-volume, folio-sized book was a collaborative achievement of great complexity. It displayed a pleasing integration of varied artisan skills. Not only did it require the services of a writer-editor, printmaker and printer, but also patrons and entrepreneurs, papermakers, toolmakers, metallurgists, bookbinders, chemists and more.

The martyrologist John Foxe called it "the miracle of printing." The *Martyrs Mirror* appeared in the springtime of printing. Instead of an earlier laborious handwritten transcribing of a martyr story, the *Martyrs Mirror* was a miracle of printing, one thousand identical copies, offered to an expanding reading public. The Mennonites of Amsterdam

were riding the wave of a radical transformation in European intellectual life.

We Muster Empathy for Rulers

We meet rulers who in those chaotic times were seeking to prevent the worlds they governed from falling apart. They saw their society as one and indivisible, with God willing one faith, one church, one clergy, one state. We learn of their deep fear that Anabaptists were destroying God's good society by disobeying their orders, not bringing their infants to be baptized, rejecting military service, refusing to swear the civic oath and worshipping separately. Anabaptists were conspirators, these rulers believed, who had to be stamped out before they could win more to their cause and thus endanger the whole body. Their concern for the maintenance of law and order led these heads of government, step by step, to the use of torture to punish, to force confession of guilt, to intimidate and silence opposition, to extract names and locations of fellow believers.

We become aware that those magistrates who killed and tortured perceived themselves to be good people, engaging in painful chores for the public good. As we seek to understand both sides in this conflict we anguish over the tragedy of good people obedient to crown and church, torturing and killing good people who claim a higher obedience.

We Develop Understanding for Dissenters

We hear Anabaptists, those without power, speaking to persons of power, explaining their heretical ways: "We must obey God rather than men. We follow the way Jesus teaches and calls: the way of humility, simplicity, peace, love and suffering. The established church is not the true church. The true church is found where Christ's disciples gather in his name. We appeal to the authority of scripture for our faith and conduct. For these convictions we are prepared to suffer and die."

Through the centuries the unyielding suffering of victims of torture has led to the emergence in British common law, as well as in other legal systems, of the principle that no one is bound to self-betrayal. The Fifth Amendment to the United States Constitution embodies this fruit of the martyrs' witness: "No person shall . . . be compelled in any criminal case to be a witness against himself."

We Are Drawn with the Expectancy of a Theatergoer

The execution of Anabaptists was high public drama—a ritual of civil religion and spectacle. This was a dramatized sermon of both divine wrath and a warning visited on dissenters. In his 1660 martyr book van Braght named it "Bloody Theatre."

The liturgy of death included all the elements of drama: a *rehearsal dinner*—where prior to some executions the magistrate gave a banquet, placing the victim in the dubious seat of honor, flanked by the magistrate and the leading cleric; a *stage*—a public place, often the town square, where people gathered; a *script*—carefully choreographed proceedings leading to the execution; a *director*—the magistrate (sheriff, mayor, prince) asserting the majesty of law and the power of office; the *cast*—an Anabaptist victim, hoping to make a "good witness," sometimes through a final statement, public prayer or the singing of a hymn; the *clergy*, standing near and poised to receive a death-moment confession, and the magistrate, symbol of authority; *stage hands*—executioner, jailor, soldier, Anabaptist-hunter; *props*—chains, stake, straw and wood for burning, rope, axe and sword, tongue screw and bag of gunpowder to insure instant death; *spectators*—good people who came to support the magistrate, enthusiasts who came to see a good show and jeer any ineptitude on the part of the executioner, supporters who quietly encouraged the victim, family and fellow believers who watched in sorrow; and *reporters* who recorded the event on public record.

We Confess Our Horror

Although inoculated with television violence, we shudder at the savagery of God's children branding, stretching, whipping, piercing, chopping, mutilating, violating the bodies of other of God's

Death-torture is the art of maintaining life in pain, by subdividing it into a "thousand deaths." . . . Death forms part of a ritual.
Michel Foucalt Discipline and Punish

children. We learn that torture, rooted in Roman law, began with psychological intimidation: threats to family, promises of more cruel torture to come, taunts to the victim with instruments of torture to be used, overheard screams of pain from unknown fellow victims, and the relentless questioning of victims who are ordered to stand erect often for hours without sleep.

Luyken captures in his etchings the banality of torture, the dreary routines. In every scene of torture and execution stand the clergy — vicars of Christ — poised to receive the victims' confessions. Vultures at the carcass.

We Admit Our Foreboding

Torture and killing of prisoners of conscience are all about us: a sister in the church whose father died in a Soviet labor camp, two employees from El Salvador who fled death squads at home, a student imprisoned for twelve years on South Africa's dreaded Robben Island. Amnesty International, recipient of the 1977 Nobel Peace Prize, reports that in the 1980s more than one-third of the world's governments used or tolerated torture of prisoners. Torture has been elevated to new levels of sophistication with electric shock, drug injections, doctors monitoring the victim's ceiling for pain. Our collective memory of torture and killing, sensitized by the stories of the *Martyrs Mirror,* should help us now to hear those screams in the night.

We Are Pursued by Difficult Questions

Why do good people torture and kill good people? Why do good people resist other good people acting for their common good? Why do modern governments continue to torture and kill? Why do the powerful fear the weak? Does anyone have the right to abuse the body of another of God's creatures? Does capital punishment dissuade potential criminals? Is the teaching to love one's enemy practical counsel? What beliefs are worth dying for? One cannot read the *Martyrs Mirror* without being haunted by difficult contemporary questions.

We Know the Strength of Story

We learn by precept and propositions. We may learn even more by parable. Jesus came telling parables, stories. The Bible is a book of stories, the story of the ways of God with his people. The New Testament tells The Story, the salvation story of Jesus. The *Martyrs Mirror* is a book of stories of faithful and faltering people who are carriers of The Story. Van Braght told martyr stories as a means of renewing the church.

During the 1740s in colonial Pennsylvania, as warfare was erupting in the west, Mennonite leaders commissioned the Ephrata Brethren to translate and publish the *Martyrs Mirror.* They hoped to recover the martyr memory, and

There is no hiding the fact that it is much harder to be a Christian today than it was in the first centuries. . . . When it becomes the "sacred duty" of a man to commit sin, the Christian no longer knows how he should live. There remains nothing for him to do but bear individual witness — alone. And where such witness is, there is the Kingdom of God.
—*Reinhold Schneider*

thereby strengthen the nonresistant resolution of their youth. Again in the 1770s, as revolutionary times swept Europe, Amishman Hans Nafziger and Mennonite Peter Weber joined forces to publish the Pirmasens edition of the *Martyrs Mirror* with the same purpose: story as a means of renewal and restoration.

We come into the presence of the *Martyrs Mirror,* and these selections from it, with thanksgiving for storytelling and with expectation that in the recovery of a martyr memory, a weary and uncertain people can renew their strength and vision.

As the flames of war appear to mount higher, no man can tell whether the cross and persecution of the nonresistant Christians will not soon come, and it is therefore of importance to prepare ourselves for such circumstances with patience and resignation, and to use all available means that can strengthen faith. Our whole community has manifested a unanimous desire for a German translation of the Bloody Theater of Thieleman Jansz van Braght . . . we consider it to be of greatest importance to become acquainted with the trustworthy witnesses who have walked in the way of truth, and sacrificed their lives for it.

Letter from Pennsylvania Mennonites to the Dutch Mennonites in Amsterdam, Holland, requesting help in translating and publishing the Martyrs Mirror, *1745*

About the Stories

We offer a series of short tales about martyrs, each one incomplete in itself. Our intention is to give a more composite picture of martyrdom—touching upon its many aspects and its much variety—than only a few stories could sustain. For each story we have therefore selected some singular, often unique, element in order to show the variety that was the sociopolitical reality for victims of sixteenth-century religious discrimination. Fuller details for each martyr are usually found in the *Martyrs Mirror* itself, or more frequently in the *Mennonite Encyclopedia*. We have chosen source material not used by either van Braght or writers in the *Mennonite Encyclopedia*.

Our selection of tales is both accidental and deliberate. We chose the stories of some twenty-three martyrdoms, illustrated by Luyken's etchings, from the thirty original plates that actually survived the ravages of war and accidents of neglect. We reproduce prints of the entire thirty. In addition, we include a few additional stories with their illustrations from among the seventy-four plates that were lost. The tangled story of the plates is told elsewhere in this book.

We arrange the stories by subject, not chronology: martyrdom as spectacle for curious onlookers, how Anabaptists were caught, how Anabaptism strengthened some families and divided others, how Anabaptist prisoners and victims were treated, how Anabaptist quarrels made their capture easier (Anabaptist martyrs were indeed heroic, but also human). We hope our arrangement of these stories provides a broad spectrum of details on the experiences of Anabaptist martyrs.

Endnotes supply citations of only obscure sources and explanations of some of the more controversial issues—especially those where we have inadequate source material and we choose to speculate.

One closing detail: in the sixteenth century, Lowlands cities or villages were identified regionally by provinces: Holland, Zeeland, Gelderland, Brabant, etc. Only in 1579, under the leadership of the House of Orange, did a cluster of northern-most Lowlands provinces begin to emerge as the nation-state we now call The Netherlands. We use the modern term, anachronistically, to make some place-names easier to locate, both in story and on the map.

Map of the Martyrdom Sites

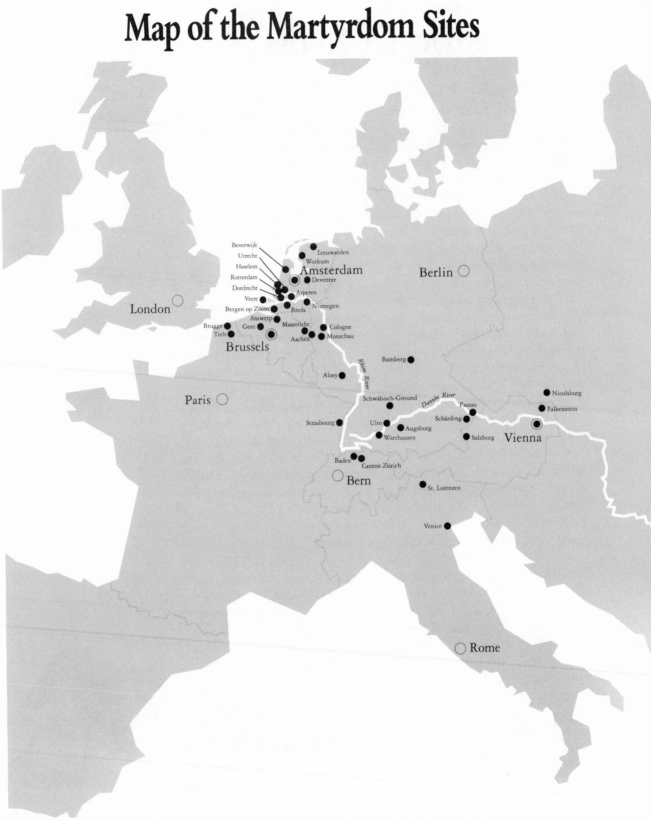

Beverwijk
Utrecht
Haarlem
Rotterdam
Dordrecht
Veere
Bergen op Zoom
Antwerp
Brugge
Tielt
Gent

Leeuwarden
Workum
Amsterdam
Deventer
Asperen
Breda
Nijmegen
Maastricht
Cologne
Monschau
Aachen

Brussels

Berlin

London

Alzey

Rhine River

Bamberg

Paris

Schwäbisch-Gmund

Danube River

Nicolsburg

Falkenstein

Strasbourg

Ulm
Augsburg
Warthausen

Schärding
Passau

Salzburg

Vienna

Baden
Canton Zürich

Bern

St. Lorenzen

Venice

Rome

The Martyrs

No.
1

Jesus Christ, A.D. 33

No.
3

Stephen, A.D. 34

Eat, Drink and Be Merry
Gerrit Hazenpoet, Nijmegen 1557

No.
67

Sixteenth-century executions were public spectacles with a moral: the state will severely punish grievous sinners in this world, and the church will consign their souls to hell in the next. Some executions were preceded with a banquet, in which the victim was forced to take the seat of honor between the mayor and the leading cleric. Such banquets appear to have originated in France and were carried to the Netherlands by their Burgundian overlords in the fourteenth and fifteenth centuries.[1] The high and mighty always ate and drank too much.

At Gerrit Hazenpoet's banquet he refused to drink any wine at all. He said he would drink the "new wine in the Kingdom of the Father," his own protest against excess and his disgust at the barbarous ritual of an innocent man being handled as a common criminal.

Hazenpoet, a modest tailor by trade, fled his native city of Nijmegen, The Netherlands. When he secretly returned to the city to visit his wife and children, a policeman recognized him. Arrested along with other Anabaptists, Hazenpoet was tortured, imprisoned for twenty-four days, then condemned to death by burning. His wife came to the city hall, probably at the conclusion of the detested banquet, to bid him farewell (the moment Luyken has chosen). She fainted from grief and had to be carried out.

The city paid out more than thirty-seven Brabant guilders to arrest, feed, interrogate and torture Hazenpoet; to purchase necessary fuel (wood and straw); to set the stake; to execute him; and finally to purchase wine for the celebrations (forty percent of the total sum was paid for this wine). The city paid money to more than twenty men for their services in some part of this network of death.[2]

At the stake Hazenpoet sang a farewell hymn to Christian brothers and sisters who were certain to be silent witnesses of his final hour.[3]

Expenses for Gerrit Hazenpoet's Execution

Here follow the amounts paid out for specific tasks and services. These are in Brabant guilders. There were 20 stuivers in a guilder, and 1 quarter of wine was worth 4 Brabant stuivers. Thirty-seven guilders today are worth about $70 US. If one compares the standard of living of that time with our own, thirty-seven guilders would be closer to $5000 US.

		% of Total
1. Police to capture him	2/14	7.3
2. Executioner to torture him	/12	1.7
Rope to torture	/ 3	.4
Executioner wine	/ 3	.4
3. Celijs van Aken to feed him 24 days	7/ 4	19.5
4. Jan van Venloe to plant the stake	/ 6	.8
5. Gaert Ketell to supply the pile (fuel)	1/ 7	3.7
6. Celijs van Aken, fagots	/13	1.8
7. City foreman to bring the straw and hay	/14	1.9
*8. Doctor Theol. Borchardt von den Berch to induce to recant	2/ 8	6.5
*9. Prior of Benedictine abbey to induce to recant	3/12	9.7
10. City foreman to take him to court	/ 3	.4
11. City foreman to take him to stake	/15	2.
12. Executioner to kill him	/15	2.
Other costs of killing	/15	2.
*13. Lords who preside at execution	14/16	40.0
Total	37/	100.1

There are records of other more broadly based charges, to capture or deal with other unnamed Anabaptists.

*1. Mayor, to Arnhem on account of Ana. [prob. to get counsel] 12 qu.	2/ 8	16.7
*2. Mayor, consults mayor of Ubbergen how deal with Ana. 20 qu.	4/	27.9
*3. Police searching for Ana., and for a non-Ana. 95 qu.	4/15	33.1
*4. **Masters of Sunter Claes (8) visit Ana. in prison, etc. 16 qu.	3/ 4	22.3
Total	14/ 7	100.0

*The payments were in wine, by the quarter at 4 stuivers per quarter. One quarter was about the measure of one bottle; approximately, therefore, one quart in our measure.

**These were men mandated to visit people in prison and attend meetings of the city council to make sure that prisoners' rights and the rights of the city were respected.

Fatal Integrity—Holy Foolishness
Simon de Kramer, Bergen op Zoom, 1553

No. 64

Simon the Vendor (Kramer) sold his simple wares under a canopy in the market square of Bergen op Zoom, The Netherlands. One day, in a lavish display of piety and authority, the local clergy carried the consecrated communion wafers in a parade through the town. When they passed Simon's stall, he refused to kneel. He had left Catholicism for the Anabaptist faith and practice, and considered bread-made-Christ sheer idolatry. His customers and fellow vendors pleaded with him to kneel down and save his life. He refused. Seized on the spot by the priest's followers as a suspected heretic, Kramer was quickly tried and sentenced to death. Within a few days he was burned at the stake in a public execution outside the city walls.[4]

Early Anabaptists were convinced that God wreaked vengeance against tyrants who shed the blood of innocents. So they repeated tales of God's wrath poured out upon some of their persecutors, including the sheriff at Bergen op Zoom. After the execution the sheriff, conscience-struck that he had killed a righteous man, began to mumble incoherently, "O Simon, Simon." Neither family nor clergy could bring him peace of mind. He died within a few days. Early Mennonite tradition compared the sheriff's fate to that of Herod, who was struck down by intestinal worms and died shortly after he had arrogantly accepted popular acclaim as God. Mennonites who continued to use the Apocrypha also compared the sheriff to Antiochus at the time of the Maccabees.

Remember the words I spoke to you: "No servant is greater than his master." If they persecuted me, they will persecute you also. If they obeyed my teaching, they will obey yours also. They will treat you this way because of my name, for they do not know the One who sent me.

—John 15:20–21 (NIV)

Betrayed by an Anabaptist Judas
Anneken Hendriks, Amsterdam, 1571

No.
87

Anneken de Vlaster, a housewife from Frisia and probably a linen weaver, was executed in a barbarous manner. The executioner tied her to a ladder, filled her mouth with gunpowder and cast her onto a bed of burning coals. At that time the Spanish garrison was terrorizing Amsterdam, attempting to check the growing Dutch national sentiment toward greater political and religious freedom.[5] However, it was rare that a woman, even a heretic, would be criminally executed by fire, rather than by drowning. Why this excessive cruelty?

Nineteen years earlier in 1552 Anneken had moved within a circle of Anabaptist sympathizers in Amsterdam. She fled the city when the authorities tightened the screws against Anabaptists. Two close friends, Aechgen Jacobsdr. and Filistis Ericxdr., were caught. They renounced their interest in the movement but were sentenced to exile despite having never been baptized. Anneken fled to Franeker in Frisia, where her interest in Anabaptism was apparently rekindled and she was baptized. She married "in the secret Anabaptist manner" (according to the court record; the ceremony was not recognized by the court).

When she returned to Amsterdam in October 1571, she was recognized by a police officer or informer whom she later denounced as a "Judas." We could assume from that name that he had been a member of her earlier circle of seekers exploring Anabaptist truth and knew her well enough to be able to recognize her nineteen years later. Exiled Anabaptists had to swear not to return, and were usually treated severely if they did return and were caught. Anneken may have violated some prior promise to respect a mandate of exile. Frequently Anabaptists denied the state the authority to exile them on the basis of Psalm 24:1: "To the Lord belongs the earth and everything in it." No human institution, they believed, could be so arrogant as to assume the right to control and regulate land, especially not in cases touching the interests of Christians.[6]

Both civic and religious officials marveled at Anneken's staunch faith — her obstinancy, as they put it. At her execution she publicly proclaimed the vengeance of the Lord against the unnamed Judas who betrayed her. Her mouth was filled with gunpowder to prevent her making a "good witness" with death-site remarks to the spectators. Luyken pictures her with mouth half open, probably because it was packed full of gunpowder.

During most of her adult life she moved in small circles of Bible-reading Christians, moving in and out of small Anabaptist groups. Later, Dutch Mennonites sang hymns based on her story.[7]

Things beyond our seeing,
things beyond our hearing,
things beyond our imagining,
all prepared by God for those who love him.
— *I Corinthians 2:9* (Revised English)

An Anabaptist Loses his Protective Cover
Augustijn, Beverwijk, 1556

No.
66

Many Anabaptists lived among non-Anabaptist friends and non-tattling neighbors. Not everyone was hostile to them. Often they were respected for their moral fervor, esteemed for their integrity. Augustijn, a baker of Beverwijk, The Netherlands, even had friends in high office.

Beverwijk's police officer, a friend of Augustijn, promised him protection. On the other hand, Beverwijk's mayor was a fanatic of the traditional faith and vowed to catch and kill any Anabaptist he could find. One day when the police official was out of town, the mayor suddenly forced other policemen to arrest Augustijn. They surprised Augustijn at his bread-board, kneading dough. Unaware of the impending danger, he had no time to escape. In a hastily convened kangaroo court, the officials quickly sentenced him to death and rushed him to a bed of hot coals before his friend could return.

At the hurriedly assembled farewell banquet Augustijn conversed with another highly placed friend, Joost Cornelissen. They said their farewells, vowing to see each other soon in heaven. No, interjected the mayor, Augustijn was destined for hell. Augustijn turned on his persecutor, sharply commanding him to appear for judgment before the throne of God within three days!

Immediately after the execution the mayor fell ill. Deranged in mind, he cried out endlessly, "Peat and wood," and died within three days.

Misfortune will bring death to the wicked,
        and punishment befalls those who hate the righteous.
The Lord delivers the lives of his servants,
        and no punishment befalls those who seek refuge in him.
                                        —*Psalm 34:21–22* (Revised English)

Anabaptist Family Networks
David van der Leyen and Levina Ghyselins, Gent, 1554

No.
65

Anabaptist missionaries spread their message among people of widely differing social and economic groups. Still it was common and entirely natural for grateful converts to share their newfound faith with members of their immediate families. So Möllers from Zwickau, Nespitzers from Passau and Kleins or Schleifferins from Augsburg, brought their blood brothers and sisters to the new faith. They were joined by their household servants as in the biblical story of Cornelius whose household accepted his faith.

Some Anabaptist families lost more than one member to the executioner's axe. One example is the van der Leyens of Gent, where a small church flourished in the late 1540s. Van Braght published an account of the execution of David van der Leyen, drawing his information from a hymn published in the earliest Dutch Mennonite martyr book, *Het Offer des Heeren.*[8]

David was burned in 1554. His sister Tanneken was drowned at Antwerp in 1555, his brother Lauwers beheaded at Antwerp in 1559. Another brother, Franchois, was caught and tried in 1558, disposition unknown; we can assume that he also was killed. The Anabaptist father of the four had an unknown end. Here was a family of courage who stood firm in torture and execution.[9]

Levina Ghyselins was burned with David, but her arrest and trial were unrelated to his. She was the wife of an Anabaptist shoemaker, Willem, who had been executed some months earlier. Her execution was postponed because of her pregnancy. After she had delivered her baby the authorities killed her, orphaning six children.

Executioners frequently bungled their work and were derided in turn by spectators in the carnival atmosphere of the bloody theater. On one occasion an executioner required seven blows with a dull axe to sever the head of one Anabaptist.[10] The executioner strangled, then burned David and Levina. After the coals had died down around David's supposedly lifeless corpse, spectators cried out that he still lived. Goaded by their jeers, the executioner plunged a large iron fork into David's breast.[11]

Unknown to each other before the moment of execution, David and Levina were united by their common fate. They encouraged each other with the promise of a blessed eternity soon to come. When the ropes were to be twisted around their throats, they commended their spirits to the Lord.

Those blessed of the Lord will live,
So Scripture teaches us.
They are driven out.
We cry out unceasingly:
Lord, take care of your
Beloved Bride, these good people,
Enfold them in your arms.
This I resolve [to beseech].

—Final stanza of the song *"Ghy Christen al te samen"* —Het Offer

Noble Family Divided
Maria and Ursula van Beckum, Deventer, 1544

No. 57

Anabaptism could also be the sword of Christ that cut families apart. When Maria van Beckum joined the Anabaptists, her mother drove her from their house. Maria fled from Frisia to her sister-in-law Ursula near Deventer, but her mother set the police on her trail. Early one morning a posse surrounded the house and routed Maria from her bed. One young, unmarried woman against many armed men, she persuaded Ursula to go with her to the arraignment and hearing. Ursula suspected that if she fell into the hands of malevolent clergymen, she herself would not be freed. She therefore won permission from her husband, Jan, to go. Maria and Jan's mother came to Deventer to dissuade both women, but to no avail. Jan gave support to neither captive, and did not appear even at their execution. Here were Catholic mother and son pitted against Jorist (an Anabaptist group) daughter/sister and daughter-in-law/wife.[12]

Love for each other and divine courage sustained the two women. They answered their interrogators crisply; both understood and explained their faith with skill, to the point of angering several clergy. Their major interrogator was called from Burgundy to induce them to recant.

They prayed for strength to withstand the fire, but also for courage to give a good witness. When the spectators wept aloud at the execution site, the two admonished them to bewail their own sins and learn the grace of God that overcomes fear and brings his children home to Him.

They radiated joy in death.

The story of their courage under family pressure made a lasting impression on many. Their tale was told in martyr books beyond the Mennonites' own, as almost no other Anabaptist's was. Perhaps their noble birth gave them higher prominence and heightened as well the inner family conflict over their Anabaptist persuasion.

Folklorists seized upon the death of Maria to fashion the story of nature itself outraged at the unjust death of a young single woman. According to the story, the next morning her badly charred stake burst forth in green foliage.[13]

We praise the Lord,
Who gives his folk from above
Such grace and strength
That brings us victory
With all the righteous
Who gain the crown.
When we came to the test
We learned with them
What they had discovered.
God be praised eternally. Amen
—*Stanza 43, Hymn No. 17,* Ausbund

You must not think that I have come to bring peace to the earth; I have not come to bring peace, but a sword. I have come to set a man against his father, a daughter against her mother, a daughter-in-law against her mother-in-law; and a man will find his enemies under his own roof.

—*Matthew 10:34–36* (Revised English)

Anabaptist Hunters Break Into a Peaceful Congregation
Hans Schmidt (or Raiffer), Aachen, 1558

No. 71

Hunters of Anabaptists generally caught them singly or in small groups. Occasionally they made a lucky catch, finding a congregation in worship and seizing all of them before any could escape. Police caught eighty-eight in Augsburg on Easter Sunday, April 12, 1528. Police broke into a small congregation of twelve in Aachen on January 9, 1558, seizing even an infant in its cradle. The civil authorities tortured the Aachen faithful by stretching them on the rack, but also suspending them by their arms and attaching heavy iron weights to their feet. One man recanted, five remained steadfast, including leader Hans Schmidt. Six women were flogged and exiled; five men were strangled and burned in October 1558.

Schmidt was a Hutterite missionary, successful at winning Swiss Brethren to his cause. He fished in troubled Anabaptist waters in the Palatinate, profiting from quarrels among them. A group led by Lorenz Huf converted, then migrated to Moravia. Schmidt traveled down the Rhine to Aachen and The Netherlands, convincing Anabaptists led by Hans Arbeiter to join. Schmidt was persuasive on issues touching the Christian's relation to the state; many found the sterner Hutterite view attractive. But some measure of his success was owing to his skill in winsomely presenting the Hutterite belief that the community of faith should not have individual rights to property. In fact, Hutterites charged the Swiss Brethren with neglecting the true scriptural calling to reject private property and live in closed communities that held property in common.[14]

Schmidt poured his boundless energies into composing hymns —at least sixteen after he had been arrested—and several dozen letters filled with details about torture, interrogations and life in prison. Isolated in individual cells, the prisoners sang loudly to cheer each other.

As leader, Schmidt was the first one executed. He made what Anabaptists called a "good witness" before a large crowd. When Anabaptist prisoners pleaded with God for strength and courage to make a good witness, they meant first to give their inquisitors good scriptural reasons for their faith and to remain steadfast under torture and, second, to call spectators to repentance at their executions. They deliberately seized upon the moment of execution as an opportunity for evangelization. Sometimes wily officials, therefore, executed them secretly.

Schmidt sang a hymn of joy as he went to his death.[15]

In you, O Father,
Is my joy,
Though I must suffer here!
Let me be scorned
By everyone
If your grace still is near!

Officials Reluctant to Execute
Joris Wippe, Dordrecht, 1558

No.
70

Joris Wippe was a good man, respected highly by his neighbors and fellow citizens in Dordrecht, The Netherlands. As a dyer he established cordial relations with cloth dealers who handled his product. When his religious views came under question, he was summoned before the city authorities. His fellow tradesmen counseled him not to flee but to trust in the goodwill of the officials. The authorities were dismayed to discover he was an Anabaptist. They hoped he would flee, and that they could avoid the unpleasant task of carrying out the imperial mandate of capital punishment. So they sent him up to the provincial capital, The Hague, hoping to have the case taken out of their hands. It did not work. Wippe was returned to Dordrecht for trial and sentencing.

Still reluctant, the officials

stalled for time. Finally they sentenced him to death because the law demanded it. Unlike the cases of most Anabaptist martyrs, no one seems to have tried to dissuade Wippe from his faith. To friend and neighbor alike his religion was valid. They were impressed with his kindness to the poor.

Repeatedly the city executioner refused to kill Wippe. Wippe had given food and other material aid to the man. Executioners were usually poor men, drawn from the lower class. For seven weeks Wippe lay unpunished in his prison within the city gate tower. Finally a soldier was found who was willing to kill the man. To avoid public outcry, the soldier drowned Wippe in a barrel within the prison. As was the custom, officials hung Wippe's corpse upside down from the public gallows at the city's edge.

What sustaining scriptures did a doomed Anabaptist find? Wippe wrote two letters, full of joy and loving admonition, to his wife, and one to the three oldest of his seven children. The three letters were filled with scripture quotations. For assurance that God cared for the helpless and for accounts of other persecuted heroes of the faith, Wippe used Psalms 34 and 128, John 15: 20–21 and II Maccabees 7. For admonitions to his wife and children he referred to Hebrews 13:16–17, I Peter 4:9, Matthew 12:42–43, I Timothy 5:10 and the counsel of Tobias to his son. He even asked his oldest son to teach the four youngest children how to read. In these and other scriptures Wippe uncovered a mosaic rich in consolation and assurance, enlivened always by joy.

"And now I charge you, Joos and Hansken, that together with Barbelken, your obedient sister, you will care for your three little sisters, and for Pierken, and teach them to read and to work, so that they may grow up in all righteousness, to the honor of God and the salvation of their souls . . . remember in the words of the apostle: 'It is more blessed to give than to receive.'"
—*Wippe letter to his children from prison, MM, 1685, II, 207; Eng., 587*

Compassion for the Enemy
Dirk Willems, Asperen, 1569

No. 82

No story of an Anabaptist martyr has captured the imagination more than the tale of Dirk Willems. Even now, Amish and Mennonites tell it to their children. Present-day residents of Willems' native village of Asperen, The Netherlands, can tell us details about his capture and death that van Braght did not know. In fact, their oral account enriches the sparse written records that were available to van Braght. The following story is largely from their account.

Dirk was caught, tried and convicted as an Anabaptist in those later years of harsh Spanish rule under the Duke of Alva in The Netherlands. He escaped from a residential palace turned into a prison by letting himself out of a window with a rope made of knotted rags, dropping onto the ice that covered the castle moat. Seeing him escape, a palace guard pursued him as he fled. Dirk crossed the thin ice of a pond, the "Hondegat," safely. His own weight had been reduced by short prison rations. His heavier pursuer broke through. Hearing the guard cry for help, Dirk turned back and rescued him. The less-than-grateful guard seized Dirk and led him back to captivity. This time the authorities threw him into a more secure prison, a small, heavily barred room at the top of a very tall church tower, above the bell, where he was probably locked into the wooden leg stocks that remain in place today. Soon he was led out to be burned to death. Tradition holds that his execution was bungled, with a high wind blowing the flames away from him, thus delaying death. Too many executioners were inept, usually to the disgust and even derision of spectators.

A few inhabitants of present-day Asperen, none of them Mennonite, seem to regard Dirk as a folk hero. A Christian, so compassionate that he risked recapture in order to save the life of his drowning pursuer, stimulates respect and memory. Recently Asperen named a street in Dirk's honor.[16]

But now, this is what the Lord says—
  he who created you, O Jacob,
  he who formed you, O Israel:
"Fear not, for I have redeemed you;
  I have called you by name; you are mine.
When you pass through the waters,
  I will be with you;
and when you pass through rivers,
  they will not sweep over you.
When you walk through the fire,
  you will not be burned;
  the flames will not set you ablaze.
For I am the Lord, your God,
  the Holy One of Israel, your Savior."

—*Isaiah 43:1–3a* (NIV)

Parting with an Infant Son
Anneken Jans of Rotterdam, 1539

No. 63

Who took care of the surviving children of martyrs? In a society that emphasized kinfolk ties, relatives usually took them in. We know of one young woman martyr, recently widowed, who carried her fifteen-month-old son to the place of execution and there offered him to anyone who would take care of him. He must have shared her prison cell for nearly two months.

Severe persecution in The Netherlands forced Anneken Jans of Rotterdam and her husband, Arent Jans de Lind, to flee to England. After his death she returned home in 1538 to settle her affairs. She was a woman of property. Arrested because she was suspected of being a religious deviant — she was singing a hymn in public — she was quickly tried, sentenced and drowned at Rotterdam, on January 24, 1539. At the site of execution she offered her son, Isaiah, together with a purse of money, to anyone who would promise to care for him. A baker took Isaiah, despite his wife's protest that their own six children were more than enough. Isaiah de Lind prospered as a brewer and later became mayor of Rotterdam. He never adopted his mother's faith.

Anneken wrote a final testament to her son, counseling him to choose and live as Jesus taught. "My son, hear the instruction of your mother; open your ears to hear the words of my mouth. Behold, I go today the way of the prophets, apostles and martyrs, and drink of the cup of which they all have drunk. . . . My child, do not regard the great number, nor walk in their ways. . . . Where you hear of a poor, simple, cast-off little flock, which is despised and rejected by the world, join them; for where you hear of the cross, there is Christ; from there do not depart. . . . Take the fear of the Lord to be your father, and wisdom shall be the mother of your understanding."

Anneken's testament is one of the most beautiful letters in all Anabaptist literature. It breathes a buoyant hope, a joy in the Christian way, with only brief reference to future suffering for the oppressors (drawn from a few of the richer phrases in the book of Revelation).

That Anneken's story is included in the *Martyrs Mirror* is an insightful commentary on differing Anabaptist groups of the time and their relationships to each other.

In the 1540s Menno Simons bitterly opposed David Joris and his Anabaptists because intense persecution caused Joris to promote an invisible church. He spiritualized the true church, locating it in each member's heart rather than in the body of believers who were, of course, visible, especially when they assembled. Menno said that was unbiblical.

Although Anneken was a Jorist, Mennonites kept alive the story of her death and testimony. Already in 1539 they printed her testament as a brochure, cast it into poetic form in Dutch and then German, and published it in the first edition of the Dutch Mennonite martyr book and in the *Ausbund*.[17]

My dearest son:
God dwells with those people
Who are despised by the world;
Join in fellowship with them.
They will direct you in the right path,
Lead you away from evil ways,
Lead you away from hell.
—*Stanzas 12 and 14, Hymn No. 18,* Ausbund

Endurance Under Torture
Ursula of Essen, Maastricht, 1570

In the sixteenth century, European judges routinely ordered torture in criminal cases. Anabaptists and others tried for religious deviancy were not exempt. Torture was based not only on Roman law and judicial procedures, but also on the commonsense expectation that criminals would more likely tell the full truth if tortured. However, in many cases involving Anabaptists, after the court had interrogated an Anabaptist prisoner without torture and recorded full answers, the officials applied torture and asked the prisoner to confirm the truth of, or enlarge upon, prior testimony. Few Anabaptists ever changed their tale or added to it under torture.

Executioners often began torture with psychological badgering: threats to kinfolk, the promise of torture and laying the instruments of torture before the victim. For routine torture they used the rack for men, the thumbscrew for women. They stretched a man upon a board or ladder, bound his feet or hands securely to the board, then tied his other extremities to a wheel that could be turned slowly, caught and held by a ratchet. A tightly stretched body could be literally pulled apart. Officials placed a woman's thumbs between two iron plates with a screw point fixed upon the base of each thumbnail, then slowly tightened them down. Both forms of torture were intensely painful. Prison reports abound with accounts of victims crying out in anguish.

Late in 1569, Ursula of Essen and her husband Arent were arrested in Maastricht during a surge of persecution promoted by the dreaded Duke of Alva, Spanish King Philip II's vice-regent in The Netherlands. Ursula and Arent and two women were subject to frequent torture in the prison: first verbal threats, then the rack. Ursula was racked twice, then suspended by her hands and flogged on her bare back. Three of the four prisoners were frequently tortured to induce them to reveal the names of fellow Christians in their recently growing congregation, but they refused. The victims held their peace. The four were burned separately so that none could offer comfort to a fellow victim. They all had their mouths tied shut with pieces of wood to prevent their singing or speaking to the spectators, some of whom complained to the Spanish officials.

All four were burned to death in huts of straw.[18]

All my enemies whisper together against me;
    they imagine the worst for me, . . .
Even my close friend, whom I trusted,
    he who shared my bread,
    has lifted up his heel against me.
But you, O Lord, have mercy on me;
    raise me up, that I may repay them.
I know that you are pleased with me,
    for my enemy does not triumph over me.
In my integrity you uphold me
    and set me in your presence
    forever.

—*Psalm 41:7,9–12* (NIV)

Joy in Death, Despair in Torture
Christiaen Janssens, Called Langedul, *Antwerp, 1567*

No. 79

"... Beloved wife, be of good cheer in all your sufferings that you have on account of me. ... Comfort yourself with the Word of the Lord. ... I have confidence in you, that you will not make me more sorrowful than I am already [by breaking under the strain of his expected execution]. I know you to be too brave for that. ... I hope that the Lord will strengthen us to the end. ... I hope to see you after this life in the eternal, where we shall part no more."[19]

Often van Braght's Anabaptist martyrs were joyful in death. Janssens wrote three letters to his wife, each filled with joy. Indeed, his principal sorrow seemed to be that her grief would be longer than his because she would live on, separated from him until she joined him in the afterlife. But his joy in prospective death takes clearer shape for us when we read

Janssens' comments on the excruciating pain of torture, on his deep anxiety that he and his co-sufferers would break and perhaps recant, or certainly suffer pain beyond endurance in tortures yet to come. "Then they racked me dreadfully, twisting off two cords. . . .[20] and poured much water into my body and my nose. . . ." His jailors allowed him to use a pillow and sheets his wife had sent, sheets that would not aggravate his severe abrasions. "We feared that we should be tortured a second time, of which we had a great dread, more than of death. . . ."[21]

In mid-1567 Janssens had been captured at a meeting of Anabaptists called to settle a dispute in Antwerp. Fluent in French, he distracted the police captain in close conversation, providing sufficient time for most of his fellow Anabaptists to escape through a rear door. Three were caught with him. All wrote letters to their wives and friends asking for small favors: a comb, a New Testament, a hymnbook, a nightcap. But their major purpose for writing was to provide comfort and seek Christian support. So they described their rackings, the ways they helped each other, and also quoted scripture passages that gave them courage. In this case, one turnkey named Pieter (Janssens told his wife to trust Pieter) was willing to make secret missions to deliver the messages and bring back gifts to the prisoners. This is amazing, because the principal purpose for torture was to learn the hiding places of the victims' families so that they too could be arrested.

The four men were eventually strangled, then burned. They were tied to stakes inside huts built of straw. The huts were set on fire when the fuel around the stakes was lighted. If strangulation first produced a coma, asphyxiation killed quickly.

They entered the huts of death singing praises to God.

"What do you expect to learn by interrogating us? We are ready to die rather than break the laws of our fathers."

As the smoke [from a son/brother being burned to death] streamed out far and wide, the mother and her sons encouraged each other to die nobly. "The Lord God is watching," they said, "and without doubt has compassion on us. Did not Moses tell Israel to their faces in the song denouncing apostasy: 'we will have compassion on his servant'"?

—*II Maccabees 7:2, 5b–6*
(New English)

Condemned to Galley Slavery
Hutterian Brethren, *Austria, 1540*

No. 55

For Anabaptists condemned to death, saying good-bye to spouses and children was one of their most harrowing experiences. Some had the leisure and literary skills to write letters from prison cells and towers. At Falkenstein castle in northeast Austria several Hutterian brothers, sentenced to the lingering death of galley rowers under Imperial Admiral Andrea Doria, gave their farewell in person to their wives and chil-

dren. Those families were then permitted to move across the border to Hutterite colonies in Moravia.

Some eighty brothers who would not renounce their faith and communitarian life were captured at their colony Steinabrunn in the Hapsburg family territory of Lower Austria. First, they were forcibly marched in bonds to the Falkenstein for interrogation under torture, then chained together by twos and marched through Austria and northern Italy to the port of Trieste. Most of them could expect to die within a few months, at most a few years, either from utter exhaustion or, ironically, from the naval battles in which they would be compelled to row the galleys.

However, aided by their guards, these German-speaking Anabaptists escaped from prison, picked their way through the Italian countryside with obvious help from sympathetic Italians, and returned to Moravia. Twelve were recaptured and never heard from again. Some of their Italian partisans converted and eventually found their way to colonies in Moravia. Anabaptists used their own persecution as a means to evangelization.

This was not an isolated incident. The Anabaptists frequently experienced sympathy from Austrian jailers, prison turnkeys, even higher officials, who found the Anabaptists' faith so compelling they refused to carry out the harsh royal orders of death to heretics. Many Anabaptists escaped prison under mysterious circumstances, and praised God for deliverance.

Hutterite poets cast the account of the eighty galley slaves into eight hymns that have survived. Hutterite chroniclers recorded the following prayer.

"O God in heaven look out upon the misery of thy poor people in these last days on earth. Have mercy upon them and help them for thy holy name's sake, for thou hast laid upon them the task of confession [faithful witness in this world]. Holy Father strengthen and enable thy people; fight for them and be their captain. Let them be heartily commended by thee, give them patience and victory in every need, and carry out thy own purpose through them to the end. O holy Father, save them and hold them in thy strong hand; O highest God, let them not be put to shame. Praise thy holy name through them, and lead them into thy truth, steadfast to the very end."[22]

Massacres at Salzburg
Matthäus Lang, Arch Persecutor, 1528

No. 52

In the early years of Anabaptism, fanatical persecutors appeared in various places, men who zealously tried to eliminate all Anabaptists and physically remove all traces of their existence. Some killed even those Anabaptists who recanted. Others tried to drive all of them out of their lands. Still others burned down the houses in which Anabaptists had held their baptisms in order to exorcise the evil, diabolical spirit.

Prince-Archbishop Cardinal Matthäus Lang of Salzburg (1468–1540) was a passionate man who wanted everyone in his land to be devoutly Catholic. He developed a savage hatred for Anabaptists, pursuing them relentlessly until he had driven almost all of them from his lands. The Salzburg archbishopric was a state with its own laws under the rulership of the archbishop.

Lang issued mandates, sent his

police on systematic searches for Anabaptists, prohibited conversations in inns and hostels about either Anabaptism or Lutheranism, forbade the employment of all strangers in any of the crafts or trades of Salzburg, and had all travelers through Salzburg examined closely by his police. His tightening net caught clusters of Anabaptists, from late 1527 through early 1528. Late in October 1527 he captured a group of thirty-two Anabaptists, including leaders Jerome of Mondsee and Eukarius Binder. He burned many of them. He ordered five recanters among them killed more humanely, first decapitating them and then committing their dead bodies to the flames.

Early in November Lang's police captured twenty-seven Anabaptists. He ordered five of them bound fast within the house where they had met, then had the house set on fire. Then he purified his land by burning down two other houses in which Anabaptists had worshiped.[23] Here a Christian prince-archbishop adopted pagan exorcism and purification ritual in order to satisfy his zeal for religious rectitude.

Surviving records reveal at least forty-one Anabaptists imprisoned in Salzburg's dungeons in 1528. None of the published reports indicates that they were killed, except for van Braght's brief account of eighteen deaths.[24]

If the world hates you, keep in mind that it hated me first. If you belonged to the world, it would love you as its own. As it is, you do not belong to the world, but I have chosen you out of the world. That is why the world hates you.

—*John 15:18–19* (NIV)

A Fugitive Congregation at Worship
Pieter Pietersz., *Amsterdam, 1569*

No.
81

From earliest times Anabaptists had to meet in secret. Pieter Pietersz., a ferryman on the Amstel River in Amsterdam, offered his boat as a meeting place. The worshipers could seem to be innocent passengers. Somehow the authorities learned that Pietersz. was an Anabaptist, probably because he took his newborn infant to a rural hiding place. One suspects that the midwife reported the birth and disappearance, and that the authorities sought out and arrested Pietersz. for his refusal to have his infant baptized.

Arrested in January 1569, he was tortured almost immediately, condemned and executed at the stake on February 26. We do not know what happened to his wife and child.[25]

Anabaptists ran an underground church, resorting to various strategies to avoid detection. They deliberately refused to learn the names of itinerant preachers, even of their own baptizers, as well as of the people who housed and fed them if they were refugees.[26] When they met strangers suspected of being Anabaptists, they offered a simple but unique greeting in order to discover if they shared spiritual kinship, something like Early Church Christians using the sign of the fish to detect fellow Christians. They worshiped in isolated places: a mill set apart from the main village; a forest five or six kilometers from Strasbourg; a larger than normal room in the rear of a conventional house; in the case of Pietersz., a ferryboat. Their leaders frequently changed hiding places in attics and innocent-looking sheds.[27] This life as fugitives took its toll, increasing believers' level of anxiety and drawing a growing number of Anabaptists toward some form of spiritualism with little interest in a physical, visible church. It was dangerous to run a visible church.

All day long they surround me like a flood;
  they have completely engulfed me.
You have taken my companions and loved ones from me;
  the darkness is my closest friend.

—*Psalm 88:17–18* (NIV)

Comradeship in Death
Willem Jansz. of Durgerdam, *Amsterdam, 1569*

No. 84

When Willem Jansz. learned, tardily, that his good friend Pieter Pietersz. would be executed in Amsterdam he quickly left his village.[28] Still, he arrived too late at the Amsterdam gate. It had been closed for the celebration. He bribed the guard to get in, arriving at the site of execution on the Dam only just in time to see his friend tied to the stake. Left on the fringes of the crowd, he mounted the steps of the weighing house in order to see and be heard. He cried out to support his friend: "Fight valiantly, dear brother."[29] He was seized immediately, tortured and tried within a few days, and sentenced and executed by burning only two weeks after the execution of his friend.

Rarely did an Anabaptist so openly invite arrest. Fellow Anabaptists witnessed almost all executions of Anabaptists, but they generally remained silent. Why this rash, foolhardy outcry, certain to be the cause of early death?

Willem lived in his isolated village, cut off—by one of the all-too-frequent divisions between Anabaptist groups—from that body of fellow Anabaptists who had nourished him. Dirk Philips had excommunicated the members of Willem's small group. The separation was painful to Willem, and in his misery he lost the normal restraints that bound an Anabaptist to public silence in the face of otherwise certain death.[30] Perhaps the spy network, craftily laid out to catch Anabaptists, had prevented him from seeing his brother in the Lord for a long time. Perhaps he thought that Pietersz. lacked the emotional strength to endure the stake, a condition that plagued other Anabaptists. In any event, his instinctive sense of brotherly love overpowered his normal caution.

In an unrelated case, Jan Quirijnsz. and Cornelis Jansz. were executed on the same occasion as Willem. That saved time for the authorities, but, more important, provided the public, eager for entertainment, with a more lavish death drama.

Do you not know:
      Have you not heard?
The Lord is the everlasting God,
      the Creator of the ends of the earth.
He will not grow tired or weary
      and his understanding no one can fathom.
He gives strength to the weary
      and increases the power of the weak.
Even youths grow tired and weary,
      and young men stumble and fall;
but those who hope in the Lord
      will renew their strength.
They will soar on wings like eagles;
      they will run and not grow weary,
      they will walk and not be faint.
—*Isaiah 40:28–31* (NIV)

A Mother's Last Words
Maeyken Wens, *Antwerp, 1573*

No. 95

"Love one another all the days of your life; take little Hans on your arm now and then for me. And if your father should be taken from you, care for one another. . . . The Lord keep you one and all." Shortly before her execution Maeyken Wens wrote to her oldest son, fifteen-year-old Adriaen, asking him to care for all of his siblings but especially her youngest son, Hans. She urged Adriaen to follow Jesus as she had done, even if it meant the temporary pain of prison and death. She hoped to see him in the New Jerusalem. From her prison in Antwerp, now in Belgium, she wrote two letters to Adriaen, two to her minister husband, Mattheus Wens, and a final letter to a minister friend, Jan de Metser. Her writings are among the most moving Anabaptist prison letters, because she revealed her own emotions as death approached.

She was pleased, even joyful, at her courage in facing hostile inquisitors in court, but also at the hope of the richer life to come. But death frightened her too. A victim waiting for execution suffered the extremes of hope and despair.

Dutch Anabaptist women counted quite a few literate members in their ranks, although the literacy rate was low in the European population as a whole. One of Maeyken's epistles is the sole surviving martyr letter in the hands of Dutch Mennonites today.

Maeyken's husband remains a mystery to us. Since she commended her oldest son to his father's teaching, it is clear that Mattheus had remained steadfast. Maeyken's letters to Adriaen suggest that her husband risked imprisonment and death. Yet she invited him to visit her in prison, with only a warning about high financial cost. How could he visit and not be arrested as a minister? Or did the question of money mean that he had fled north to the relatively safer provinces that became the United Netherlands, and that traveling south to Antwerp would be expensive? Neither court records nor Maeyken's letters help us on these questions. Mattheus' absence at her execution suggests that he fled for his life.

Her children were safe from arrest. Adriaen was drawn to the place of his mother's execution, carrying his youngest brother, Hans, with him. But at the moment of truth he fainted, reviving only after her body had been destroyed by fire. In anguish he searched the ashes and found the tongue screw used to prevent her own "good witness." It too survives in Dutch Mennonite hands.[31]

Remember those earlier days after you had received the light, when you stood your ground in a great contest in the face of suffering. Sometimes you were publicly exposed to insult and persecution; at other times you stood side by side with those who were so treated. You sympathized with those in prison and joyfully accepted the confiscation of your property, because you knew that you yourselves had better and lasting possessions.
—*Hebrews 10:32–34* (NIV)

53

Saintly Salt in Wound
Leonard Bernkop, *Salzburg, 1542*

No. 56

Leonard Bernkop was captured at Salzburg. Refusing to recant under torture, he was executed by a slow fire with none of the more humane techniques designed to kill quickly. Throughout the entire process his faith kept him in high spirit. At the stake he even ridiculed the hangman's helpers: "Turn me around; my side nearest the fire is roasted enough and the other remains undone."[32]

Bernkop's taunt has to have been a reference to the death of a saint long popular in that region — Saint Lawrence. Even today in that region, which has since become part of Austria, there are many shrines dedicated to St. Lawrence, many paintings of his agony. Lawrence, a deacon in the Early Church, literally was grilled to death on a gridiron in Rome in 258 AD, three days after his bishop had suffered a similar fate. Midway through the gruesome killing he jocularly reproached his tormentors: "I am roasted enough on this side; turn me over and eat."[33] To paraphrase Bernkop's taunt: "You kill us now with that same barbarity that Rome killed those early Christians whom you revere for their courage." Anabaptist martyrs were not above rubbing salt into the wounds of their persecutors.

I sought the Lord's help; he answered me
     and set me free from all my fears.
They who look to him are radiant with joy;
     they will never be put out of countenance.
Here is one who cried out in his affliction;
     the Lord heard him and saved him from all his troubles.
The angel of the Lord is on guard
     round those who fear him,
     and he rescues them.

          —*Psalm 34:4–7* (Revised English)

Anonymity of Anabaptist Martyrs
Seven Killed at Schwäbisch Gmünd, 1528

No. 53

Many Anabaptists remain anonymous to us, a few even in death. The execution of seven Anabaptists at Schwäbisch Gmünd in 1528 reminds us that many records were destroyed or never properly kept. Even though the seven each composed a stanza for a hymn that survives, we know the names of only two of these martyrs. The group included an unnamed fourteen-year-old boy, one of the youngest of all Anabaptist martyrs. His youth attracted notice from the onlookers, including a noble who — with the promise of an income for life — tried to induce the boy to recant. The lad refused. From among a group of at least forty Anabaptists, the boy and his six co-martyrs, including a woman, were the only ones to remain steadfast against appeals to recant.

The anonymity of the Gmünd seven should remind us that our

information about Anabaptists is far from complete. There may have been hundreds of Anabaptists who did not excite enough attention to enter any kind of record. Surviving court records give us ample evidence of hundreds of anonymous Anabaptists, remembered by fellow believers who did not know their names.[34]

Each of the Gmünd seven composed a prayer, repeated at the execution probably as their form of "good witness." Probably the seven cast those prayers into metric form while lying in prison. There they would have had enough contact with each other to decide on a common poetic form.

This hymn was included in the first full edition of the *Ausbund* in 1583. Since each stanza bears its own distinctive character, it is obvious that each was written by a different person, not all of them by some later editor. Four cry to God for help, two of them in some fear in the face of a painful death. One prays for the persecutors. Another asks God to strengthen the faithful (an appeal made poignant by the prior recantation of most of the congregation). One thanks the Lord for making them his ministers.

The reader cannot detect which stanza was written by the woman, or which by the boy. It was not uncommon for Anabaptists to console themselves in prison by composing and singing hymns. The more than sixty Anabaptists imprisoned for four and one-half years in Passau after 1535 composed at least fifty-three hymns.

O Lord, Thou art our Shield,
We turn to Thee.
For us it is a minor pain
When they take our lives.
In Eternity Thou has prepared for us,
So when we suffer shame and stress here
It is not for nothing. [We will be amply repaid]
—*Stanza 6, Hymn No. 61,* Ausbund

Zürich Persecutors of Mennonites Succeed
Catherine Müller, *Canton Zürich, 1637*

No. 104

Despite intervention by their Dutch brothers and sisters, Mennonites in Canton Zürich finally left their homes for other places because of severe repression. In this last wave of persecution no one was killed. The last Anabaptist-Mennonite martyr in Switzerland was Hans Landis, executed in Canton Zürich in 1614. Twenty years later, Zürich decided to compel Mennonites to return to the state church. Zürich repeatedly arrested them, imprisoned them for years at a time, confiscated their property, and declared all Mennonite marriages null and void and all Mennonite children illegitimate. Dutch Mennonites induced the city governments of Amsterdam and Rotterdam and the Dutch States-General to press Zürich diplomatically for relief. Finally Zürich let Mennonites emigrate. Sometimes persecutors succeeded in ridding their lands of Anabaptists/ Mennonites.

After a new census in 1633, four Mennonite leaders were arrested and imprisoned in December 1635. Felix Urnne escaped; the other three (Rudolf Egly, Ully Schmidt, Hans Müller) lay in the Zürich city prison for twenty-two weeks. Formal discussions proved fruitless. The Mennonites readily agreed that God called them to obey the government, but they refused to attend the state church.[35] They demanded freedom of religion, and on that issue no agreement was possible. In 1637 Zürich arrested most of the Mennonites, perhaps three hundred adults. Luyken has chosen this dragnet for his etching, singling out the figure of Catherine Müller, about whom we know nothing. Many Mennonites escaped prison, probably aided by friends. In 1639 Zürich increased the pressure. Still the Mennonites did not yield. Subsequent attempts were equally fruitless.

Finally, after the Thirty Years' War had ended (1648) and German princes sought farmers for their depopulated lands, Zürich Mennonites emigrated, taking with them some of their personal goods. Most of them went to the Palatinate, some of them on to North America.

Friends of Mennonites helped them escape prison, and also pressed others not to buy Mennonite property put up for sale by the Zürich government.[36]

You brought us into prison
    and laid burdens on our backs.
You let men ride over our heads;
    we went through fire and water,
    but you brought us to a place of abundance.
        —*Psalm 66:11–12* (NIV)

Apostolic Poverty
Arnold of Brescia, 1155

No.
42

Arnold of Brescia was an early opponent of the wealth and political power of the pope and lesser clergy. Born and raised in Brescia, Italy, he studied in France with Abelard, the most brilliant mind of the twelfth century, and took on some of his master's sharp criticism of the clergy. Several towns expelled this priest, and some bishops excommunicated him for preaching eloquent sermons attacking high-living bishops. He preached even in Rome. There he favored the senate over the papacy as rightful ruler of Rome.

Arnold taught and practiced "apostolic poverty." He thought churchmen must give up worldly power and wealth and live in poverty as Jesus' disciples did. In his view, priests who owned material goods forfeited their salvation. All clergy should live entirely from tithes regularly paid to the church by layfolk. The church should own no land. His views on a simple life for the clergy connected him with a people called the Humiliati. They were priests and layfolk who wore coarse clothing, usually of one color. Later in that century they influenced Waldenses and Franciscans toward simplicity of Christian life.

A renewed papacy under Eugenius III and then Adrian IV lay in wait for Arnold, caught him finally and burned him to death in 1155. They scattered his ashes in the Tiber River to prevent enthusiastic followers from preserving any bones as relics.

Probably it was his views on aspostolic poverty for clergy and layfolk that endeared him to Anabaptist, early Mennonite and other Protestant writers.[37]

Again I looked and saw all the oppression that was taking place under the sun:
 I saw the tears of the oppressed —
  and they have no comforter;
   power was on the side of their oppressors —
   and they have no comforter.
    And I declared that the dead,
     who had already died,
      are happier than the living,
       who are still alive.

—*Ecclesiastes 4:1 – 2* (NIV)

"Kill Them All; The Lord Knows His Own"
Medieval Crusade Against Southern French Heretics

No. 44

In the thirteenth century an unholy alliance of the papacy and French crown carried out a crusade against so-called heretics in southern France. They ravaged an entire region and destroyed a brilliant civilization. Church and state determined to destroy all adherents of the Cathari faith, killing indiscriminantly whenever they captured a major military stronghold. Indeed, this crusade brought a cynical comment from one papist leader, when soldiers and priests balked at killing because they were unable to distinguish heretics from Christians among the captured citizens of one city: "Kill them all; the Lord knows his own."

The Cathari, or "pure," believed that the power of evil and darkness equaled the power of good and light. They drew as much from Zoroastrianism as from Christianity for their doctrines and practices. A few *perfecti* separated themselves from the large body of faithful, the *credentes,* and practiced the strictest moral living. They ate no meat but also no eggs or fish. They remained single for life. They were to be completely honest with everyone. Christians in southern France found them attractive because they were morally superior to fellow Christians, especially the clergy. Some of them lived in the city of Albi and were called Albigenses, the name used by van Braght.

By 1200 the new pope, Innocent III, determined to launch a crusade to wipe them out. He used Cistercian monks to preach the crusade, and his successors turned a new monastic order of traveling preachers, the Dominicans, to that end.[38]

Church leaders together with French nobles and knights from the north poured down upon the helpless inhabitants of many cities in southern France, stormed city walls, inevitably slaughtering almost everyone. In 1210 the killing of Cathari began. By 1243 several hundred of them had retreated to Montségur, a fortress in the Pyrenees Mountains. The besiegers promised life to all defenders if they would surrender two hundred *perfecti,* a promise no one believed. After bitter fighting the attackers seized the stronghold and executed several hundred *perfecti* by tossing them alive into a huge fire.

The crusaders installed northern nobles to rule those southern people who survived, though thoroughly cowed. They imposed the northern French language and culture on the rich indigenous *langue d'oc* culture. This crusade sticks in Western memory as one of the most savage destructions of people and culture in Western history.[39]

No. 47

Trial by Ordeal
Conrad of Marburg and the Waldenses, 1214

No.
45

Could human beings induce God to intervene in human affairs, especially to judge men and women accused of false belief or practice? From the fifth to the twelfth centuries Christians used "trial by ordeal" to ask God to help decide. In such a trial the accused person underwent harsh physical tests in fire or water, and God was asked to use the test to show guilt or innocence.

Churchmen were trying to be fair, not cruel. They recognized their own inability to read people's minds or to know the inner workings of their hearts. How could earnest churchmen detect religious error in their people? Ironically and unknowingly, in their use of trial by ordeal they fell back on a practice used in pagan religions to call the gods to help them be just. They changed only the gods, not the superstition.

Trial by hot iron was one of the

cruelest ordeals. Usually the victim was compelled to walk on seven, nine, ten or twelve (each a sacred number) red-hot plowshares. Sometimes the accused carried a heated iron by hand a specified distance. Then the judge bandaged and sealed the hands or feet, probing for injuries after three days. If the hands or feet remained unburned, the victim was declared innocent.

Early in the thirteenth century Pope Gregory IX appointed Dominican monk Conrad of Marburg to be the first Inquisitor General for the German people. Conrad zealously sought the support of German princes, some of whom wanted the pope to stay out of their religious affairs. Conrad tried to convict one resisting prince, failed and died in 1233 from an assassin's knife. Earnest Christians whom he persecuted, such as the Waldenses, held him in bitter memory.

Van Braght repeated the tales about Conrad without singling out individual Waldenses who suffered at his hands.

Who has measured the waters in the hollow of his hand,
    or with the breadth of his hand marked off the heavens?
Who has held the dust of the earth in a basket,
    or weighed the mountains on the scales
and the hills in a balance? . . .
Surely the nations are like a drop in a bucket;
    they are regarded as dust on the scales;
    he weighs the islands as though they were fine dust.
          —Isaiah 40:12, 15 (NIV)

Lollards: An Underground Church
William and Joan White, *Norwich, England, 1424*

No.
49

Before the Reformation there were evangelical people who opposed what they considered the wickedness of the Roman Church. One loosely organized group in England, nicknamed the Lollards, opposed transubstantiation, celibacy for clergy, prohibitions against studying Scripture, and other commonly held beliefs and practices. They met secretly in private homes to read the Bible, ran a successful underground church and occasionally preached in the open. When the English crown rested on a minor, young Henry VI, some of them openly preached their religion, boldly denouncing the wealth and privileges of the Roman clergy.

William White was such a preacher. Ordained a priest, he had converted to Lollardy, married and traveled around parts of England calling the pope "Antichrist," denouncing pictures in the churches as idolatrous, and announcing that God alone, not the church, offers forgiveness of sins. Caught, tortured and sentenced to death, White was preparing to preach to the spectators at his execution by burning when a police officer struck him so savagely on the mouth that he could not speak.

His holy life lingered in the memory of other Lollards, sustained by the religious ministrations of his surviving wife, Joan. Religious groups such as the Lollards often relied on the religious insights and preaching of women, as the Roman Church refused to do. Joan White "taught and sowed abroad, confirmed many men in God's truth," and thereby suffered much from the bishop.[40]

They will ban you from the synagogue; indeed, the time is coming when anyone who kills you will suppose that he is serving God.

—*John 16:2* (Revised English)

The Waldenses
Dulcinus and Margaret, Novara, Italy, 1308

Jan Luyken (inuenit et fecit.

No.
48

One pre-Reformation, anti-Catholic religious group has survived to our time—the Waldenses, or Vaudois as they call themselves in northwestern Italy. Probably Peter Waldo was their founder. He began to preach "apostolic poverty" for all Christians, not only for the clergy as Arnold of Brescia had done.

In the 1170s around Lyon, France, Waldo's followers called themselves the "poor men of Lyon." They pitted the authority of the Bible against the church, translating it from Latin into the language of their people. They followed the words of Jesus in the Sermon on the Mount, at first rejecting all killing, later taking weapons to defend themselves in their mountain hideouts against the fury of their persecutors. They preferred a lay authority to that of ordained clergy, angering the Roman churchmen who declared them heretics in 1184.

Their simplicity of life attracted many, drawing perhaps upon the earlier Humiliati (and Arnold) and similar groups, and inspiring similar movements later under different names. In the 1190s Francis of Assisi founded a movement of apostolic poverty and the simple life. The Church eventually accepted his "Franciscans." It had gained wisdom from its over hasty rejection of the Waldenses. Waldo and his followers had tried to remain within the Church. In 1532 the Waldenses joined the Reformed Church.

In 1305 the papacy, harrassed by French king Philip IV, moved from Rome to Avignon in southern France. That first French pope, Clement V, set about to maintain papal authority in Italy by lashing out at religious dissidents. He unleashed a wave of killings and other persecutions of Waldenses settled on the plain and in the valleys of northwestern Italy. One of their ministers and his wife, Dulcinus and Margaret, were caught and killed at Novara in 1308. Later martyrologists, such as van Braght, reported their deaths. No surviving records of that time give us any details.[41]

They gave a great cry: "How long, sovereign Lord, holy and true, must it be before you will vindicate us and avenge our death on the inhabitants of the earth?" They were each given a white robe, and told to rest a little longer, until the number should be complete of all their brothers in Christ's service who were to be put to death, as they themselves had been.
—*Revelation 6:10–11* (Revised English)

He broke the fifth seal, and I saw beneath the altar the souls of those who had been slaughtered for God's word and for the testimony they bore.
—*Revelation 6:9* (Revised English)

69

Two Waldensian Weavers Make Demands
Hans Kager and Hans Speyser, *Augsburg, 1524*

No.
50

Some Christians objected to the Roman Church's practice of distributing the Lord's Supper in the consecrated bread only. The Church refused to permit layfolk to drink the consecrated wine, because it feared that their excitement at handling and drinking what was thought the true blood of Christ would cause them to spill some, desecrating the sacrament and thereby Jesus Christ Himself. Clergymen always laid the bread, in small wafer form, within the open mouth of each communicant. Clergy could be expected not to drop and thereby desecrate the "body of Christ."

The Waldenses and other late medieval religious protesters demanded the right to commune "in both kinds." In some towns and villages large crowds of layfolk rallied against the Church on this issue, sometimes rioting when the government authorities refused them their religious demands. Hans Kager and Hans Speyser, two Augsburg Waldensian weavers in their sixties, made this simple demand, and a riot broke out. The government seized them, quickly tried and beheaded them secretly to avoid a fresh outburst from rebellious townsfolk. For his final time Kager relented and received the sacrament in one kind only, the bread. Speyser steadfastly opposed receiving the Lord's Supper unless it was distributed in both kinds. He died "without *viaticum*," a condition normally considered terrible but one that did not disturb his view of his relation with God.[42]

A poet cast the final prayer of Kagen and Speyser into a hymn. Although printed in the *Ausbund* among other places, the hymn is no longer sung by the Amish.

We must suffer shame,
Because we do not
Oppose Thee.
If we sinned a little,
Worshiped idols [bread and wine of the Lord's Supper]
They would not harm us.
Hear us, O Lord; grab Your sword:
Judge all those men who here
Lightly assess your Might.

—Stanza 6

O God, in all Thy Majesty:
Hear Thou our
Prayer most graciously.
Because we suffer anxiety, stress,
Do not desert us;
Increase our patience,
Through Thy Son, our Captain;
To whom be honor and glory — He fights
Satan and his army. Amen.

—Stanza 14, Hymn No. 40, Ausbund

A Lutheran Martyr
Leonhard Kaiser, *Schärding, 1527*

No. 51

Leonhard Kaiser of Schärding, Bavaria, was a Lutheran chaplain martyred by Catholics in August 1527. Because Lutherans found princes and city councils to support their religious position, generally they could remain within the safety of their territories. Only a few were caught and killed. Charles V, the Catholic emperor, was determined to use his Spanish army to mend the religious division. But he could not break away from other political fights to bring his army to Germany until 1546, when the Reformation had found too solid a footing to be overturned. Killing Lutherans wholesale would have precipitated an all-German war.

Kaiser was caught in Catholic lands, interrogated and prosecuted by an earnest theologian, tried by an overzealous bishop and killed reluctantly by a bungling executioner. His steady faith and calm acceptance of death made a deep impression on many onlookers. He had a popular following, and therefore his ultimate judge, Duke Wilhelm of Bavaria, wanted to execute him in secret. But the crowd demanded its morbid entertainment.

At the place of execution, Kaiser forgave his executioner who asked for pardon. He comforted the crowd, prayed the Lord to sustain and strengthen him, then asked his followers to sing the hymn "Come, Holy Spirit." Despite the kindling of a fresh load of wood, the flames did not consume his body. The executioner crudely maneuvered his corpse with a lance and then cut it into pieces—a grisly scene.

Luther used the execution to plead against death for religious dissenters. Within three years he reluctantly agreed to death for Anabaptists in order to halt their growth.

Van Braght and earlier Anabaptist narrators[43] thought Kaiser was an Anabaptist. Perhaps one of them read his statements on baptism. He accepted the Lutheran view of baptism as sacrament, but wrote extensively about baptism of the believer, who could expect only cross and suffering—an Anabaptist theme.[44] The earliest record bears no evidence to support the legend that the flowers picked by Kaiser remained fresh and unsinged on his corpse after the second fire burnt itself out.

"In the historical conflict in which the martyr finds himself, his deed is word and his word, deed."
—*from H. von Campenhausen,* Die Idee des Martyriums in der alten Kirche *(Gottingen: 1964)*

Persecutors' Furious Last Gasps —
The Early Church

No. 32

The most barbaric of all the major persecutions in the Early Church was named for Emperor Diocletian (A.D. 284-304). From Nero (54-68) to Diocletian the Romans persecuted Christians intermittently with varying severity. In the two systematic, empire-wide persecutions (under Decius [249ff.] and Diocletian), Rome developed degrees of harassment, ultimately ending in death. Rome destroyed churches, burned Bibles and other Christian books, and turned finally to Christians themselves.

In Diocletian's persecution Christians had to sacrifice to pagan gods or be killed. Rome racked, skinned, beheaded, burned, drowned, starved or crucified Christians (sometimes head down), or used wild beasts to kill them. Executioners sometimes fastened each leg to a branch of a young tree, tied down each branch and then suddenly released both branches to tear apart the body of a Christian. Rome could always invent novel ways to kill people. Christians were not spared its cruelties any more than common criminals. Savage brutality and empire-wide intensity gave Diocletian's persecution its notorious place in history.

Some Christians developed a taste for martyrdom. For example, when the first edict against Christianity was publicly posted in the eastern capital, Nicomedia, a young Christian named Euethius tore it down. The authorities seized and executed him for treason before the day was over. And at public executions in the amphitheater, almost always attended by other Christians not yet arrested, some Christians in the crowd voluntarily came forward to beg for the executioner's axe.[45]

Why kill Christians? Christianity had hundreds of thousands of adherents including imperial officers, especially in the eastern parts of the empire. It might have even been dangerous to attack them there. Sensing the steady decline of the empire, Diocletian set out to destroy anarchic elements that threatened to tear Roman society apart. Some of his counselors persuaded him that Christianity, a brash new religion that would not adapt itself to any pagan religion tolerated by Rome, seriously dampened public spirit and destroyed Roman citizens' allegiance to the state. Christians revered another God, not the god of the state.

The best Roman minds always regarded any divinity as power. The Christians' God would not kowtow to Roman power and therefore had to be eliminated from the hearts of His adherents. Diocletian began the ten-year persecution, then eighteen months later resigned his office and practiced his hobby, raising cabbages. His co-emperor, Galerius, and a subsequent emperor, Maximin, were the most brutal executors of the persecution. Yet even they had to surrender to the victorious martyr spirit of the Christians. In 311 Galerius issued Rome's first decree of religious toleration of Christianity, and finally asked Christians to pray to their God for him in his fatal illness.

Less than a century later, Christianity, by then the only legal state religion, began to persecute followers of pagan religions. Ironically, in 525 a pagan Roman senator wrote one of Western civilization's most eloquent pleas for religious toleration — against Christian persecutors.

No.
58

A Failed Anabaptist Jailbreak
Eight at Amsterdam, 1549

No.
61

Humiliated in Death
Two at Bamberg, 1550

A Burning of Books that Backfired
Three at Haarlem, 1557

Joy in Suffering
Algerius, Rome, 1557

No.
74

Caught Reading the Bible
Andries Langedul, Antwerp 1559

No.
88

A Bungled Execution
Wolfgang Binder, Scharding, 1571

Scriptural Fluency from an Illiterate
Hendrik Eemkens, Utrecht, 1562

Hendrik Eemkens, an illiterate tailor from East Frisia, successfully used his vast store of memorized scripture to counter the arguments of the clergy who tried to persuade him to recant. Luyken has depicted Eemkens' executioner firing a bag of gunpowder hung around his neck before burning his body. Killing with gunpowder was thought to be more humane than the slower burning to death.

The Artist: Jan Luyken, Printmaker, *1649–1712*

Jan Luyken was a premier Dutch printmaker in the generation following Rembrandt. He designed more than 3,000 copper plates to illustrate histories, Bibles and his eleven books of religious verse. A man of gentle, pious spirit, he fellowshipped with Mennonites and Collegiants. One hundred and four of his etchings appear in the 1685 edition of the *Martyrs Mirror.* Thirty of these copper plates survive today.

Jan Luyken was the fifth child of a humble, devout Amsterdam couple of Remonstrant faith — Casper Luyken and Hester Corres. Jan's fa-

ther, a good friend of the revered Mennonite minister, Galenus Abrahamsz. de Haan, was a self-taught schoolteacher who tutored his son through elementary studies. The family encouraged Jan's emerging artistic talents with lessons in painting from Martinus Saeghmolen. He gained his first recognition, however, as the author of amorous verse, *The Dutch Lyre,* which intimates that he had a less than pious youth.

In 1675 at the age of twenty-six, married and with children, Jan Luyken experienced conversion. He was described as "aglow and inflamed by the love of God."[1] He celebrated his new spiritual joy with a series of

thirty-nine poems, published in 1678 under the title, *Jesus and the Soul.* A Dutch literary critic called these poems, "one of the greatest lyrical works in our literature. A masterpiece, whole in its composition, a description of the soul moving back to God step by step, with firm resolve, with surprises which bind and fuse."[2] Historian Irvin B. Horst characterized Luyken's piety as "a Jesus-spiritualism with an emphasis on fellowship with Christ and following in His footsteps."[3] He perceived himself primarily as a poet, with his graphic art in a supporting role.

At the age of twenty-eight, Luyken appears to have abandoned the painter's brush for the etcher's needle. Like Rembrandt before him, Luyken followed procedures still used today by printmakers. A copper plate is covered with a thin acid-resistant ground of asphalt, resin and wax. Lines are drawn with a needle in the waxy ground, thus exposing the metal underneath. When the plate is immersed in an acid bath, the acid bites into the plates on the lines exposed by the needle, thus creating U-shaped grooves. The printmaker inks the plate, then wipes the plate clean of excess ink, leaving only the ink lodged in the lines and crevices. Dampened paper is placed on the plate and pressure applied with a hand-operated press, forcing paper into the inked grooves on the plate. The paper then bears the reverse image of the printmaker's copper plate.

Luyken first revealed his gift as a printmaker with forty etchings illustrating *Jesus and the Soul,* published by Pieter Arentsz., a Mennonite bookseller in Amsterdam. His book illustrating one hundred trades and professions, published in 1694, has endured in popularity to this day. In 1681 he contributed an etching of Menno Simons for the complete works of Simons that has been called "Menno with the Open Bible." The scripture is open to Matthew 5:39, the passage about turning the other cheek. His 340 large etchings illustrating *The History and Figures of Scripture* (1712) have a Breughel-like scale and mastery of detail. The Dutch translation of *Pilgrim's Progress,* illustrated by Luyken, enjoyed long life as a best-seller.

In 1682 Luyken's wife died. Thereafter he chose a life of poverty and asceticism. From this period came his *Spiritual Letters,* published posthumously. By 1689 Jan began to collaborate in printmaking with his son Caspar, who died in 1708, four years before his father.

Jan Luyken, who illustrated more than 500 books in his lifetime, spent his last years quietly working in his printmaker's studio, living simply, helping the poor and providing spiritual aid to friends and strangers. A portrait of Jan Luyken from the year of his death, 1712, bears a caption by Spinniker: Luyken's "soul rising to God, but lingering in his verse and art to beckon us to God."

When Luyken was commissioned to illustrate the 1685 edition of van Braght's *Martyrs Mirror,* he had illustrated more than ninety books. He contributed 104 plates[4] that appeared in the large folio work. (One which he submitted for the title page was rejected in preference to one by I. van der Vinne.)

Luyken, who lived close to the age of the Anabaptist martyrs, was probably granted freedom to select stories that captured his artistic eye and moved his spirit. One marvels at his sensitivity to detail and his portrayal of the serenity of martyrs crossing the mystic boundary between life and death. Avoiding a focus only on the high drama of execution, Luyken probed perceptively the martyr experience in its varied light and shadow.

Clearly Jan Luyken was gifted as a printmaker with superb technical skill. His contemporaries appear to have valued his etcher's talents, when one considers the major projects for which he was commissioned. We wonder whether Luyken's humility or his piety may have contributed to the fact that his work has been largely neglected by keepers of artistic taste. Now three centuries later we encounter a gifted artist whose time for study and recognition has again come.

An artist of monumental productivity: more than 3,000 etchings. And yet he was a modest man who brushed aside praise. Of his art he said, "It serves me only as a staff to sojourn in the present country."[5] Jan Luyken was both poet and artist, but also pilgrim.

The Author: Thieleman Jansz. van Braght, *1625–1664*

Thieleman Jansz. van Braght wrote and published the *Martyrs Mirror* in 1660 because he thought the Mennonite church of his time needed the witness of its fathers and mothers who had courageously died for their simple faith.

He did not lay bare the flaws of his fellow Mennonites for us. We must speculate. In his time some Mennonites had become wealthy. Intellectuals among them had introduced rationalist elements into their religion. Still others had enlivened the earlier Anabaptist spiritualism, some to the point of caring little for a visible church. Others had entered almost every branch of Dutch cultural life in that century of heightened Dutch cultural vitality. Surely there is no other time or place in all of Mennonite history when Mennonites participated so fully in every aspect of a vigorous national culture as these seventeenth century Dutch Mennonites did. But more than a trickle of his fellow believers were leaving the Mennonites, choosing religious persuasions more sympathetic to their cultural and intellectual interests. Van Braght probably found each of these emphases exaggerated, believing that they were detrimental to that purer, more biblical faith that he cherished.

He had to have been disturbed by the War of the Lambs, that factional struggle originating in Amsterdam but spilling out into other Mennonite centers. As a conscientious preacher in the Lamist church, he had to have known the bitter pain that its divisions caused. He was regarded by fellow Mennonites at the Lamist church as a conservative who nevertheless could mediate between groups.

In any event, he ruefully reported that there were some who would never accept anything that he wrote. He decided to write, therefore, for the well-disposed, as he put it. He offered to discuss his findings with others, even to the point of altering his printed work if proven wrong, as long as his health permitted.[1]

Van Braght was born in 1625 in Dordrecht, the son of a cloth merchant, whose trade he followed. He studied foreign languages, including ancient tongues, after the pattern of his countrymen. At twenty-three he became a Mennonite preacher, an office he occupied until his death in 1664.[2] His arguments with some Dutch Reformed preachers, together with his thorough, century by century, treatment of the subject of baptism in the *Martyrs Mirror,* suggest that it was that topic that informed and guided his private study of church history and theology.

Van Braght wrote several books, the *Martyrs Mirror* requiring massive research, the others less so but still demanding enough. He did all of this while still young. He was in his early thirties when he researched and wrote his *Martyrs Mirror,* which was published when he was only thirty-five. He died at thirty-nine. In so short a life span his accomplishments were monumental.

Van Braght's work breathes a spirit of moral earnestness, above all in the *Martyrs Mirror.* But it lives in his *School of Moral Virtue,*[3] a book directed to young people, exhorting them, in standard Mennonite religious fervor, to be good. Its final, eighteenth, edition was published in 1824. The same spirit is present in his *Fifty-One Sermons on Varied Scripture Passages*[4] and in some of his hymns. Van Braght was a devout Mennonite who wanted to revive and pass on that biblical simplicity of earnest moral living that he found in early Anabaptists.

Here we are interested primarily in his *Martyrs Mirror.* One is astonished at his unlimited capacity for hard work, at the passion with which he constantly searched for new sources about his martyr subjects. He was indefatigable, writing much of the book from his sickbed.

How accurate was he? What was the quality of his scholarship?—a fair question in view of his own defensiveness on the point.

As a scholar he was extremely careful with his sources. For example, he began his study intending only to reprint the last prior Mennonite martyr book,[5] then found its authors omitting too much documentary evidence and making too many factual errors. So he wrote to many archivists, found much new material, especially within court records, then filled holes and corrected errors in earlier martyr accounts. His writing is characterized by a passionate attention to detail that is almost fussy. He tried always to be scrupulously correct. He understood how difficult it was to be accurate, then declared, finally, that he was certain he had made some errors. His integrity deserves applause.

As an example of his painstaking care with detail, take the case of Joris Wippe, drowned in Dordrecht in 1558. Van Braght scoured the city archives to find the official death sentence. He uncovered, finally, the names of all nine judges who passed sentence on Wippe. Then he decided he could not be certain that they voted unanimously to kill him, since they had tried to pass on the case to The Hague in order to avoid carrying out the capital offense law of the land on Anabaptists. Van Braght's historical scholarship is exemplary for his times, more than a century before the advent of a genuinely critical approach to history.

Still, his work will not satisfy the demands of twentieth-century scholars. He accepted too naively some accounts taken largely from oral sources. He did indeed make errors. Above all, he did not deal with those Anabaptists who chose not to be killed. In so doing, he failed to tell a truly balanced story of the times.[6] All the same, his is a remarkable tour de force on important aspects of life and death in sixteenth-century Netherlands.

The Lost Plates Are Found

Jan Luyken's 104 copper plates used in the 1685 *Martyrs Mirror* had disappeared. Last seen by Mennonite historians in south Germany in 1930, the plates were thought to have been destroyed during World War II or perhaps melted down as scrap metal in wartime Germany. In 1975 thirty of the lost plates reappeared. Seven plates were purchased by American Mennonites but twenty-three slipped into the hands of a Rhineland art collector. For thirteen years, despite repeated inquiries, no word could be obtained about the twenty-three plates.

In late May 1988, Amos Hoover, Old Order Mennonite historian from Lancaster County, Pennsylvania, phoned Robert Kreider of North Newton, Kansas, to report that the lost had been found! The German art collector had died and the plates he owned were available for sale. Soon John Oyer of Goshen, Indiana, joined in the effort. Ten months of negotiations followed.

On an April Saturday morning in 1989, around a table in a coffee shop in Grünstadt, Germany, a group gathered to unwrap rever-

Lost and Found . . .
Once there were 104 Luy-
ken copper plates.
Now there are 30.
Where are the other 74?
Sold for scrap in wartime?
Forgotten on an attic shelf?
Unidentified in museum
storage?
Taken as souvenirs by
occupation troops?

ently and carefully each of the twenty-three plates and to examine the delicately etched artistry of Jan Luyken. Here were the works of art by a Mennonite poet and printmaker who sought to revere with skill and affection the memory of his Anabaptist martyr ancestors, who lived only a few generations before. In outline this is the odyssey of the lost copper plates:

1685 — In Amsterdam, Jan Luyken's 104 copper plates were used in the printing of the second edition of the *Martyrs Mirror.* Luyken's plates were used fully or partially in Dutch printings of the book in 1698, 1715 (?), 1732, 1738 and 1762.

1778 — Hans Nafziger, Amish bishop from the German Palatinate, secured the plates for a German printing of the book at Pirmasens in 1780. He collaborated in the project with his Mennonite friend, Peter Weber. This edition used the German translation prepared by the Ephrata Brethren on the Pennsylvania frontier.

1880 — A Rotterdam newspaper reported that Luyken's plates were discovered in a chest in the home of Ed Heim, a railroad official from Lambrecht in the Palatinate.

1925 — Mennonite historians Christian Hege of Frankfurt and Christian Neff of the Weierhof learned that ninety plates were in the possession of a Christian Wolf of Munich. Hans Weber, Sr. of Munich ac-

quired the plates at the time of Wolf's death. The disappearance of fourteen plates has never been explained.

1930 — Harold S. Bender and Neff, Mennonite historians, saw the ninety plates, but in those Depression years could not afford the approximately $2000 purchase price.

1944 — Hans Weber, Jr., who had inherited the plates on the death of his father, moved with his family to a forest retreat as Allied bombing intensified. He left behind the ninety plates hidden in three boxes of building supplies at his firm in Grünstadt, Germany.

1945 — American soldiers occupied the Weber home and building supply business.

1969 — Amos Hoover visited the Palatinate seeking the lost plates. He found no trace.

1975 — Hans Weber, Jr., owner of the plates, died. One box of thirty plates was rescued while workers were clearing a storage area in the family business. Each plate was wrapped in newspaper and covered with bricks and tiles. Weber's children offered to sell the plates to a nearby Mennonite pastor, who told them of Hoover's earlier search. "Providential" is Hoover's word for the letter carrying the news that the plates could be purchased.

1977 — Following two years of negotiation, Amos Hoover purchased seven plates from Thomas Weber, the late

Hans Weber's son. However, twenty-three plates slipped out of his grasp into the hands of an art collector by the name of Lamberts, in the Rhineland. Retaining two plates, Hoover sold five plates to interested persons and institutions. Hoover encouraged Robert Kreider, North Newton, Kansas, to persist in efforts to secure the twenty-three plates. These inquiries met with silence.

1988—Thomas Weber informed Amos Hoover that the art collector had died, the plates were again for sale, and the Weber family had no interest in repurchasing them. Hoover phoned Kreider. There followed letters, cables, phone calls and visits and, through it all, a plodding series of negotiations. John Oyer of Goshen, Indiana, joined in the quest, followed soon by Gary Waltner of the Weierhof, Germany, and Willy Hege of Altkirch, France.

1989—Twenty-three plates were purchased in Grünstadt on behalf of Mennonite patrons.

Once there were 104 Luyken copper plates, now only thirty. Where today are the other seventy-four? Sold for scrap in wartime? Forgotten on an attic shelf? Unidentified in museum storage? Discarded in a city dump? Taken as souvenirs by occupation troops?

Thirty plates have survived wars, plundering and neglect to carry the memory of martyrs long past, but living still.

Endnotes

Endnotes for pages 20–75

For abbreviations, please see the Bibliography for a full citation of the work.

1. Hoog, 192. Johan Huizinga, *The Waning of the Middle Ages: A Study of the Forms of Life, Thought and Art in France and the Netherlands in the XIVth and XVth Centuries* (London: Edward Arnold, 1948), *passim*, has excellent illustrations of this practice. Van Braght does not mention banquets or meals prior to execution. But he has numerous verbal final encounters between victim and either ruling clergymen or major government officials—occasions for the Anabaptist to warn of impending divine retribution, for instance. Many of these can be visualized as occurring, not necessarily at the site of execution, but at a prior meeting where there was much more leisure to discuss matters of innocence or the judgment of God. Hazenpoet was captured and killed in 1557, not 1556 as van Braght has it.

2. P.C.G. Guyot, *Bijdragen tot de Geschiedenis der Doopsgezinde te Nijmegen* (Nijmegen: Vieweg, 1845), 19–23. Simon Schama, *The Embarrassment of Riches* (Berkeley: University of California Press, 1988), 617, reports that in the seventeenth century 200 guilders was the annual salary of a Reformed pastor.

3. "Oorlof aen Broeders en Sisters gemeen" ("Farewell to all brothers and sisters"), *MM*, 560.
"Brothers, sisters, all, good-bye!
We now must separate,
Till we meet beyond the sky,
With Christ our only Head:
For this yourselves prepare,
And I'll await you there."

4. Our only source of information on Kramer is van Braght, who was not able to find the official court records.

5. Jan Wagenaar, *Amsterdam in zyne Opkomst, Aanwas, Geschiedenissen, Voorregten, Koophandel, Gebouwen, Ker-kenstaat, Schoolen, Schutterye, Gilden en Regeering . . .* (Amsterdam: Yntema en Tieboel, 1760–[1794]), I, 321.

6. P. Sijbolts, "De Doopsgezinden te Middelburg in de 16de eeuw," *Doopsgezinde Bijdragen,* 1908, p. 51; Grosheide, 183–84.

7. A hymn was written about her, "Ick moet u nu gaen verclaren, Watter t'Amsterdam is geschiet," and published in *Veelderhande Liedekens.*

8. "Ghy Christen al te samen," *Het Offer,* 534.

9. A. L. E. Verheyden, *Het Gentsche Martyrologium (1530–1595)* (Brugge: De Tempel, 1946), 20–21, who lists other van der Leyens who may well have been relatives: Lievin in 1534, Merelbek in 1551, and Jan with no date given.

10. Van der Haeghen, I, xv.

11. Not intestines, as Luyken's print would have it. The term used in the sources, *bust,* is a south Netherlands word for breast.

12. The sharp division in the family shows most clearly in the *Ausbund* account, Hymn No. 17.

13. The Zürich Zentralbibliothek owns a non-Mennonite broadside picturing the stake of execution sprouting green leaves, together with a poem describing the event. The van Beckum execution was recounted by Ludwig Rabus. As a Lutheran he normally excluded stories of Anabaptist martyrs.

14. Hutterian Brethren practiced community of goods, permitting no member to own material goods of any kind. They established the practice in 1529 in Moravia, reestablished it more firmly in 1533 under Jacob Hutter from whom they took their name. Sixteenth-century Moravia was a rare sanctuary, permitting Anabaptists to live together in communal societies. Hutterites proselytized other Anabaptist groups, including those called Swiss Brethren, arguing a superior scripture-based life on this issue and that of stricter discipline of all mem-bers. Approximately 25,000 Hutterterian descendants of these early Moravian colonists live in North America today.

15. See *The Chronicle,* 354–63, for many details drawn from his letters, most of them addressed to his "sister in the Lord," his wife. See *Die Lieder,* 551–611, for Schmidt's sixteen extant hymns, one with 112 stanzas.

16. Dirk's pursuer acted on his own authority. There was no mayor, or anyone else, standing at the edge of the pond urging the guard to seize the prisoner. See Leroy Beachy, "Unser Leit," *The Budget* (Sugarcreek, Ohio), Nov. 16, 1988, p. 10, for his interesting account of gathering information about Dirk from residents of Asperen in the summer of 1989. In May 1990, John and Carol Oyer gathered additional details from both Asperen's Reformed preacher and also the town's regional historian. The latter, Jan van Leerdam, has combed various archival records and found fresh information unavailable to van Braght. Van Leerdam presently promotes the story among Dutch of his region, in part because he is appalled at authorities of the sixteenth century killing people for religious reasons only. In many villages the Spaniards killed Dutch patriots who resisted their rule. Seldom did they kill for religion only. Van Braght discovered the 1606 archivist's transcription of the judicial sentence. He also reported oral accounts of the excessive pain caused by the executioner's bungling. The story has attracted interest in other quarters; for example, see H. Tollens Czn., *Nieuwe Gedichten,* for a poem. See also ten Cate, I, 78.

17. Anneken wrote a letter of comfort to David Joris. See Nippold, "David Joris von Delft," *Zeitschrift f. die historische Theologie,* XXXIII (1863), 3–166; XXXIV (1864), 483–673; XXXVIII (1868), 475–591. Also ten Cate, I, 42. Recently a novel was written about her life: M. van der

Staal, *Anneke Jansz.: Historische verhaal uit den eersten tijd der hervorming* (Urk: de Vuurtoren, 1976).

18. Torture of these four was especially brutal, for no special reason. The Dutch regarded it as the cruelty of the Spanish. Neeltgen, a woman of 75 and the mother of Trijntgen, another of the four, was not racked because of her age. Three hymns describing these events are included in that rarest of Anabaptist hymn books, *Ein schon gesangbüchlein.*

19. *MM,* 705.

20. Apparently the executioner stretched the rope so tightly that two strands of the rope broke. Janssens' joints were almost separated so that he had to be carried to his bed after torture. Van Braght found many letters from prisoners to spouses and friends. But few of them have so much detail about torture, or are filled with such ecstatic joy. *MM,* 705.

21. *Ibid.,* 707.

22. Aldo Stella, *Anabattismo e anti-trinitarismo in Italia nel XVI secolo: Nuove ricerche storiche* (Padova: Liviana, 1969), 258–68; Grete Mecenseffy, ed., *Österreich, I. Teil,* Quellen zur Geschichte der Täufer, XI (Gütersloh: Gerd Mohn, 1964); *Die Lieder,* 89–115; Josef Beck, *Die Geschichts-Bücher der Wiedertäufer in Österreich-Ungarn* (Vienna, 1883; reprint, Nieuwkoop: de Graaf, 1967), 654.

23. See Lang's excessively cruel mandates, Nov. 1527 and April 18, 1528, in Greta Mecenseffy, ed., *Österreich, II. Teil,* Quellen, XIII (Gütersloh: Gerd Mohn, 1972), 20–24. See also Paul Dedic, "Lang von Wellenberg, Matthäus," *ME,* III, 286–87.

24. Our own research indicates that Mecenseffy did not find or publish all of the existing records of Anabaptists in Salzburg's archdiocesan archives.

25. We have only the story as told by van Braght, who uncovered and printed the city's official account of the sentence and death but found no details on the manner of execution.

26. Augsburg was a city with Anabaptists who hosted other Anabaptists from neighboring or distant regions for many months. In court trials these alien prisoners repeatedly could not name their hosts, but only indicate where they lived. Nor could they name those craftspersons—seamstresses, cobblers, etc.—who employed them for months on end. They could identify only craft and residence.

27. See Gary Waite, "Staying Alive: The Methods of Survival as Practiced by an Anabaptist Fugitive, David Joris," *Mennonite Quarterly Review,* LXI (1987), 46–57.

28. Durgerdam was a small village at the edge of Amsterdam, called Doornickendam in the sixteenth century. It is part of Amsterdam now.

29. Grosheide, 180, using records from the Amsterdam archives.

30. *Ibid.,* 180–81; Kühler, I, 395–426, for an account of the schism.

31. Some scholars have denied Maeyken's existence because court records failed to mention a Maeyken Wens. Samuel Cramer identified her as Maeyken of Dissenbeke, whose name does appear in the records; Dissenbeke was her place of residence. Her husband had worked there as a mason. She was executed, along with three other women, on October 6, 1573. Van der Zijpp, "Maeyken Wens," *ME,* III, 439–40; Cramer, in *Doopsgezinde Bijdragen,* 1898, p. 114; 1899, pp. 104, 108, 121; 1904, pp. 115–33 (espec. p. 127). See also van der Haeghen, II, No. 841.

32. Beck, 151.

33. "Assum est, versa et manduca," which John Foxe, I, 93, translated: "This side is now rosted enough, turne up O tyrant great; Assay whether rosted or raw, thou thinkst the better meat."

34. For this account one needs to balance data from four sources, some of which draw upon other sources that have not survived. (1) *Ausbund* Hymn No. 61; four Hutterite hymns in *Die Lieder,* 48–59; Gustav Bossert, "Gmünd, Schwäbisch," *ME,* II, 528-30; *MM* II, 433–34. Van Braght quoted an unnamed source, one who reported from the Anabaptist perspective but very likely an earlier oral tale written down only later. Van Braght had the seven executed in 1529, but the court records used by Bossert in his *ME* article indicate an execution date of December 7, 1528. The *Ausbund* believed all of the seven to be males. Bossert's court records told him that one was a woman.

35. The fullest account is *Ein wahrhaftiger Bericht von den Brüdern im Schweitzerland, in dem Zürcher Gebiet* (1645), probably written by Hans Müller or Jeremias Mangold for the Dutch Mennonites. Van Braght used this material extensively. Since 1742 it has been reprinted in every North American edition of the *Ausbund.*

36. The fullest account is Cornelius Bergmann, *Die Täuferbewegung im Kanton Zürich* (Leipzig: Heinsius Nachhf., 1916).

37. Ludwig Rabus (Lutheran), Adriaen Haemstede (Dutch Reformed) and Jean Crespin (French Reformed) included Arnold in their martyr books, the latter only as a presumed Waldensian. The Humiliati later became a semimonastic order. Arnold held no formal tie with their predecessors, but some church historians link him with them.

38. The Dominicans are a monastic order founded by Dominic in 1218, named the Order of the Preachers. Popes generally found their inquisitors within this order, until these monks were sometimes nicknamed the "hounds of the Lord" (in Latin, *domini canes*) and pictured by contemporary artists as white hounds with black spots, since they wore white robes covered on occasion by black mantles.

The Inquisition was a special detection and trial system used by the church to detect and punish heretics. Set up around 1215 by Pope Innocent III, it was run by churchmen appointed by the pope. Testimony against the victim was often anonymous; even the indictment was not often revealed to the victim. Torture was freely used. The church delivered convicted victims to the political authorities for punishment, almost always death.

39. Van Braght read historians of his time who thought the Cathari might have been Waldenses. He thought the Waldenses much closer to a pure and righteous historical church than the Cathari, even though

he revered the Cathari for their moral superiority over the Roman Church. Waldensian historians, such as Comba, have long held that all Waldenses had been driven out of these southern French regions into the mountain retreats of northwestern Italy (Piedmont at that time). It is van Braght's insistence on a group of 200 victims in 1243 that makes one certain they were the 200 Cathari of Montségur, a connection that Enea Balmas reported in 1975. See Emilio Comba, *History of the Waldensians of Italy* (Eng. trans.; London, 1889); Amedeo Molnar, *Storia dei Valdesi,* 3 vols. (Torino: Claudiana, 1974); Anonymous, *Storia delle persecuzioni e guerre contro il popolo chiamato valdese. . . ,* ed. and trans. (from French) by Enea Balmas (Torino: Claudiana, 1975). Adriaen Haemstede, Dutch Reformed martyrologist, included these 200 victims in his book of martyrs, calling them Albigenses, not Waldenses; van Braght ignored that evidence apparently.

40. Foxe, I, 869, 871–72.

41. The origins of the Waldenses are shrouded in mystery because only scant records survive those earliest years. Those records are universally hostile and therefore not fully credible. The possible derivation of Waldenses from prior groups, Humiliati or Patarini or others — together with possible relation to the Cathari who were clearly heretical by any historian's judgment — are matters of conjecture. The Waldo connection seems reasonably clear. Subsequent persecutions were so numerous that details about particular victims generally were lost.

I find no mention of Dulcinus and Margaret, or of Waldenses at Novara, in the latest standard histories of the Waldenses: Amedeo Molnar, *Storia dei Valdesi,* I (Torino: Claudiana, 1974); Jean Gonnet and Amedeo Molnar, *Les Vaudois au moyen age* (Torino: Claudiana, [1974]). Neither author was trying to cover all persecutions.

Van Braght and some other Mennonites of his time believed that the Waldenses were not so much forerunners as founders of the Anabaptists.

42. This account is taken primarily from an Augsburg chronicler of the early sixteenth century. Friedrich Roth, ed., *Die Chronik von Clemens Sender,* Die Chroniken der deutschen Städte vom 14. bis ins 16. Jahrhundert, XXIII (Leipzig: Hirzel, 1894), 159. Gustav Uhlhorn, *Urbanus Rhegius* (Elberfeld, 1861), 62, used Sender and also the minutes of the city council to record the same data. Van Braght followed earlier martyr accounts in using the names Hans Koch and Leonhard Meister for Kager and Speyser. *Meister* is the German word for "master," as for example "master weaver": i.e., a weaver who has graduated through the stages of apprentice and journeyman, finally producing his "master" work acceptable to the guild and thereby licensed to make and market woven goods. Neff, "Koch, Hans," *ME,* III, 210, decides for unexplained reasons that Kagen is not the accurate name for Koch; Hege, "Kager, Hans," *ME,* III, 135, uses the earlier name with an ending "r" rather than "n," but does not identify him with Koch. I prefer the earliest accounts.

43. *The Chronicle,* I, 54–55; Beck, 25–26.

44. Rabus, II, 162v.

45. Many Christians followed the counsel of leaders such as Cyprian, who advised them to flee persecution. It would come to them in due time, as it did for Cyprian himself. Christian writers Eusebius, later bishop of Caesarea, and Lactantius, both of them eyewitnesses of some of the more gruesome events, have given us the most vivid descriptions. Despite their exaggerations, most historians find their accounts credible because of the commonly recognized cruelties of Roman governments. Eusebius, *History of the Church from Christ to Constantine,* trans. G. A. Williamson (Baltimore: Penguin Books, 1965); Lactantius, *De mortibus persecutorum* (On the Deaths of the Persecutors), in Lactantius, *The Minor Works,* trans. Sister Mary Francis McDonald, The Fathers of the Church, LIV (Washington, D.C.: Catholic University of America Press, 1965), 119–203. See also Philip Schaff, *History of the Chris-*tian Church* (rev. ed.; New York:

Endnotes for pages 80–82

1. Irvin B. Horst, "Jan Luyken: Devout Poet and Printmaker," *Eastern Mennonite College Bulletin,* February, 1976, p. 3.

2. Dick Coster, "Joannes Luyken," *De Stem,* 1927, p. 645, cited by Horst, ibid., p. 3.

3. ibid., p. 6.

4. In a later edition, collaborating with son Casper, Luyken added eleven prints of more recent martyrs. These are etchings of lesser quality.

5. Horse, p. 4.

Endnotes for pages 83–84

1. pp. **** r., v., 1660 edit.; p. 19 of Eng. edit.

2. Van der Haeghen, 49; see also H. Westra, N. van der Zijpp, "Braght, Tieleman Jansz van," *ME,* I, 400–01.

3. *De Schole der zedelijcken Deught, geopent voor de Kinderen der Christenen* (n.p., 1657).

4. *Een-en-vyftigh Predicatien, over verscheyde Schriftuer-plaetsen . . .* (Amsterdam: Jan Rieuwertsz, 1670).

5. Hans de Ries et al., *Historie der Martelaers ofte waerachtige Getuygen Jesu Christi . . .* (Haarlem: Daniel Keyser, 1615). Van Braght refers to this as the "old book."

6. See the careful assessment of van Braght's scholarship, S[amuel] Cramer, "Die Geloofwaardigheid van van Braght," *Doopsgezinde Bijdragen* (1899), 65–164.

Endnotes for pages 85–87

1. Amos B. Hoover, "Jan Luyken's Lost *Martyrs Mirror* Engravings," *Pennsylvania Mennonite Heritage* I (January, 1978), 2–5. Correspondence in possession of Robert S. Kreider and John S. Oyer.

Bibliography

Ausbund. Das ist: Etliche schöne Christliche Lieder, wie sie in dem Gefängnis zu Passau in dem Schloss von den Schweizer-Brüdern . . . gedichtet worden. (n.p., 1564; Lancaster County, Pa.: Amish Congregations, 1984).

Thieleman J. van Braght, *The Bloody Theater or Martyrs Mirror of the Defenseless Christians,* trans. Joseph F. Sohm (Scottdale, Pa.: Mennonite Publishing House, 1984). Cited as *MM.*

Steven Blaupot ten Cate. *Geschiedenis der Doopsgezinden, in Holland, Zeeland, Utrecht en Gelderland* (Amsterdam: van Kampen, 1847).

The Chronicle of the Hutterian Brethren, I, trans. and ed. by the Hutterian Brethren (Rifton, New York: Plough Publishing House, 1987).

Jean Crespin, *Le livre des martyrs* (Geneve: Crespin, 1554). Expanded as *Histoire des martyrs persecutez et mis a mort pour la verité de l'Euangile* ([Geneve: Eustace Vignon], 1582). The 1619 edition was reprinted in 3 vols. (Toulouse: A Chauvin, 1885–89). French Reformed.

John Foxe, *Actes and Monuments of the Latter and Perillous Dayes . . .* (2nd ed.; London, 1570). Anglican.

Het Offer des Heeren, 1570 edition, Samuel Cramer, ed., Bibliotheca Reformatoria Neerlandica, II (The Hague: Nijhoff, 1904).

Greta Grosheide, *Bijdrage tot de Geschiedenis der Anabaptisten in Amsterdam* (Hilversum: J. Schippen Jr., 1938).

Ferdinand van der Haeghen, et al., *Bibliographie des martyrologes protestant Néerlandais,* 2 vols. (The Hague: Nijhoff, 1890).

Adriaan van Haemstede, *Historien oft Gheschiedenissen der vromer Martelaren* (n.p., 1559). Revised and enlarged by Joannes Gysius, as *De Historie der Martelaren . . .* (Amsterdam: Weduwe van Schipper, 1671; reprint, Utrecht: Hertog, 1980). Dutch Reformed.

W. J. Kühler, *Geschiedenis der Nederlandsche Doopsgezinden in den 16e Eeuw,* 2 vols. (Haarlem: Tjeenk Willink, 1932–1950).

Die Lieder der Hutterischen Brüder (Scottdale, Pa., 1914; reprints: Winnipeg, Man., 1953; Cayley, Alta., 1962, 1974).

The Mennonite Encyclopedia, ed. Harold S. Bender et al., 4 vols. (Scottdale, Pa. and Newton, Kans.: Mennonite Publishing House and Mennonite Publication Office, 1955–1959). Cited as *ME.*

Ludwig Rabus, *Historien, der heiligen ausserwölten Gottes Zeügen, Bekennern, vnd Martyrern, so zum theyl . . . ersten Kirchen . . . zum theyl aber zu disen vnsern letsten zeytten. . . .* (Strassburg: B. Beck Erben, 1552–56). Lutheran.

Ein schon gesangbüchlein Geistlicher lieder, zusamen getragen Auss dem Alten und Newen Testament Durch frome Christen und liebhaber Gottes . . . (n.p. [probably Rhineland, n.d. [1563–65]).

Veelderhande Liedekens, ghemaeckt wt den Ouden ende Nieuwen Testamente (n.p., 1569).

A. L. E. Verheyden, *Anabaptism in Flanders, 1530–1650* (Scottdale, Pa.: Herald Press, 1961).

Suggestions for Further Reading

Myron S. Augsburger, *Faithful Unto Death: Fifteen Young People Who were not Afraid to Die for their Faith* (Waco, Texas: Word Books, 1978).

Victor G. Doerksen, "The Anabaptist Martyr Ballad," *Mennonite Quarterly Review,* LI (1977), 5–21.

The Drama of the Martyrs, Intro. Jan Gleysteen (Lancaster, Pa.: Mennonite Historical Associates, 1975).

Cornelius J. Dyck, "The Suffering Church in Anabaptism," *MQR,* LIX (1985), 5–23.

Dave and Neta Jackson, *On Fire for Christ. Stories of Anabaptist Martyrs Retold from* Martyrs Mirror (Scottdale, Pa. and Kitchener, Ont.: Herald Press, 1989).

Alan Kreider, " 'The Servant is Not Greater than His Master': The Anabaptists and the Suffering Church," *MQR,* LVIII (1984), 5–29.

Jan Luiken: Printmaker, 1649–1712, Eastern Mennonite College *Bulletin,* February, 1976.

James W. Lowry, *In the Whale's Belly and Other Martyr Stories* (Harrisonburg, Va.: Christian Light Publications, 1981).

"A Martyrs' Mirror Digest," *Mennonite Life,* XXII (April 1967).

"The Martyrs Mirror: Some Essays," *Mennonite Life,* XLV (September 1990).

Gerald C. Studer, "History of the *Martyrs' Mirror,*" *MQR,* XXII (1948), 163–79.

A. Orley Swartzentruber, "The Piety and Theology of the Anabaptist Martyrs in van Braght's *Martyrs' Mirror, MQR,* XXVIII (1954), 5–26, 128–42.

About the Authors

John S. Oyer teaches European and Mennonite history at Goshen College, Goshen, Indiana, beginning in 1955. He did his graduate study at Harvard University, the University of Chicago (Ph.D.) and Heidelberg University. In 1964 he authored *Lutheran Reformers Against Anabaptists* (The Hague: Nijhoff). Since 1966 he has edited the *Mennonite Quarterly Review,* a journal of Anabaptist/Mennonite history.

For his research activities he and his wife, Carol (Schertz), and their four children have resided for longer periods of time in Germany, Austria and Switzerland. Since 1949 he and his wife have been members of College Mennonite Church, Goshen, Indiana.

Robert S. Kreider is an educator (Ph.D., University of Chicago) who has taught history and peace studies on the faculties of Bluffton (Ohio) College and Bethel College, North Newton, Kansas. He has served as an academic dean and college president. Kreider has frequently traveled abroad on assignments for the Mennonite Central Committee, Mennonite World Conference and China Educational Exchange. Recently he retired as Professor of Peace Studies and Director of the Kansas Institute for Peace and Conflict Resolution. Among other writings he edited *The Anabaptist-Mennonite Time Line* (Faith and Life Press, 1986).

Kreider and his wife, Lois, live in North Newton, Kansas, and are members of Faith Mennonite Church. They are the parents of five children.